STOP THE CLOCK

TOM JACKSON

STOP THE CLOCK

RED LEMON PRESS

First published in Great Britain by
Red Lemon Press Limited
Northburgh House,
10 Northburgh Street,
London, UK EC1V 0AT

For Windmill Books Ltd

Designer: Phil Gamble
Picture Researcher: Sophie Mortimer
Editors: Dawn Titmus, Tim Harris
Editorial Director: Lindsey Lowe
Design Manager: Keith Davis

ISBN 978-1-78342-005-6

A CIP catalogue record for this book is available from
the British Library.

Printed and bound in China by HangTai.

1 3 5 7 9 8 6 4 2

www.redlemonpress.com

Red Lemon Press Limited is part of the
Bonnier Publishing Group
www.bonnierpublishing.com

CONTENTS

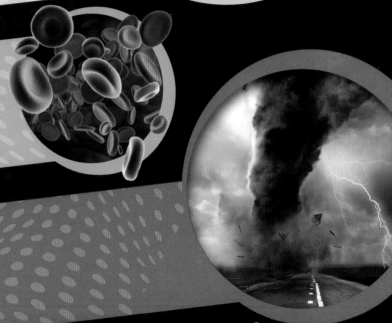

STOP
THE CLOCK!

It's time to explore record-breaking facts about what's happening every second, minute, hour, day and year on Earth. Uncover the record number of cockroaches slurped down in one minute. Hold your nose and find out how much gas a cow lets out each day. How many years does it take to walk all the way around the world? Every second, incredible things are taking place across the globe. What could have happened in the minute it took to read this paragraph? The clock is ticking – read on to find out!

SECONDS

60

SECONDS 13

The world record chicken flight lasted just 13 seconds! Chickens spend most of their time on the ground. They fly only to escape danger.

1 SECOND

The Sun burns off four million tonnes of gas every second. But don't worry – there's enough gas to keep the Sun burning for billions of years.

HOT!

60

SECOND 1

Every second, 6,750 sq m of rainforest is cut down. That's almost the size of a football pitch!

An avalanche is a wave of snow weighing as much as ten million tonnes. Don't get in the way! The fastest avalanches can hurtle down a 1,000m slope in just 12 seconds.

12 SECONDS

The Google search engine answers 54,000 search queries every second! And it does that in 146 different languages.

SECOND 1

Takeru Kobayashi of Japan must have been hungry on 25 March 2011. He managed to eat a bowl of pasta (weighing 100g) in just 45 seconds – the fastest time ever.

45 SECONDS

10 SECONDS

Every ten seconds, 40 carats (about 8g) of diamonds are dug up from the world's mines. Most of them are tiny chips of sparkling crystal. Stones bigger than one carat (0.2g) each are much more rare.

60

Bu^zz^zz!

 54 SECONDS

In 2011 Ben Lee from the UK played the song 'Flight of the Bumblebee' in just over 54 seconds, making him the world's fastest violinist. To finish in that time, he had to play 15 notes every second!

If you stepped on a pin, you'd feel it in 0.02 seconds. That's how long it takes for the signal to reach your brain.

SECONDS **0.02**

 14 SECONDS

It takes 14 seconds for water to plunge from the top of Angel Falls to the bottom. The waterfall in Venezuela is the world's highest at 979m – three times as high as the Eiffel Tower.

SECOND 1

The clay models in a *Wallace and Gromit* movie are adjusted by only tiny amounts at a time to create all the action. In every second of the final film, the characters make 24 minuscule movements!

SECONDS 2

The shortest BASE jump (jumping off an object using a parachute) was made by Austrian Felix Baumgartner. In 2001 he jumped off the 29m-high arm of the Christ the Redeemer statue in Rio, Brazil. He had less than two seconds to open his parachute before hitting the ground.

What do you get when you combine basketball and trampolines? The answer is slamball, one of the fastest sports around. Slamball teams have just 15 seconds to take a shot at the basket, or the ball goes to the other team.

SECONDS 15

SECONDS 0.5

Facebook users upload 1,500 photos every half a second. In the same amount of time, 15,625 other people will have left a comment.

STAYING IN TOUCH

People have invented dozens of ways to chat. Every second there are billions of phone calls and other messages being sent around the world. What are we all saying?

The first e-mail was sent in 1971. You could say the invention was a success! In the next 30 seconds alone 100 million e-mails will fly around the globe.

SECONDS 30

SECOND **1**

In 2012 34,700 telephone calls were made in the USA every second. That means one person out of every 9,000 Americans was dialling a number for every second of every day.

In just five seconds we send a million texts, or SMS. U wud get sore fngrs if U tried dat urself!

SECONDS **5**

SECOND **1**

Every second, 72 minutes of new video is added to YouTube, where users watch 4 billion hours of video clips every month.

Posted letters are sorted automatically by machines that can read the address – even bad handwriting. The fastest mail sorters can process 15 letters every second.

SECOND **1**

True or false

A blog is a personal website where people can write about whatever they want. The Google blogging service publishes one million new words every 22 seconds.

(Answer on page 32)

In 2006 a group of 400 skydivers met up in mid-air over Thailand and formed the largest skydive formation ever. They held the record-breaking position for just under five seconds.

SECONDS 5

60

cLick!

SECONDS 9.58

In 2009 Usain Bolt became the fastest man in history when he ran 100m in just 9.58 seconds. That's the length of seven school buses.

1 SECOND

Grasshoppers are noisy little critters. They rub their legs together to make loud, creaky calls. The insects' back legs have little pegs on them, which click when scraped over each other. One second of calls contains about 7,300 clicks.

Every two seconds, 11 tonnes of sugar are produced around the world. That is 1.25 million teaspoonfuls.

SECONDS 2

You are not supposed to play with your cutlery but we can make an exception for Aaron Cassie of Winnipeg, Canada. In 2009 he spent 30 seconds with 17 spoons balanced all over his face – including his ears. That must have taken some practice!

SECONDS 30

Every second, three Barbie dolls are sold around the world. That is an incredible 94 million every year.

SECOND 1

1 SECOND

Lightning is an enormous electric spark that is created when masses of air rub together inside a swirling storm cloud. The electric charge builds up inside the cloud until it floods out as a flash of lightning. Every single second, 45 bolts of lightning are striking somewhere around the world.

SECOND 1

Dolphins communicate using squeaks and whistles. Each call is made up of thousands of clicking sounds. The dolphin's voice produces about 2,500 clicks in one second.

Hello!

The fastest speed skater in the world is the Canadian Jeremy Wotherspoon. He can complete a 500m circuit in 34 seconds. That means he skates more than the length of a railway carriage every single second!

SECONDS 34

The speediest lifts in the world are being installed in the Shanghai Tower, a 632m-high skyscraper being built in China. When finished, the lifts will take people from the ground to the 121st floor in less than 35 seconds.

35 SECONDS

Every second, 4,671 cans of soda – fizzy drinks like lemonade or cola – are being drunk in the United States.

SECOND 1

60

American David Smith Jr launched into the record books in 2011 when he fired himself out of a cannon live on Italian TV – hurtling to a world-record-beating 59.05m in just three seconds.

SECONDS 3

SECONDS 27

Eric Barone is the fastest man on a bicycle. In 2002 he rolled down the Cerro Negro volcano in Nicaragua, taking just 27 seconds to reach 172km/h. That's the take-off speed of a small aircraft.

IN A HEARTBEAT

Every second, over 7 billion human hearts thump all around the planet – including yours. These facts will have your heart racing in no time!

30 SECONDS

The average resting heart rate of an athlete in tip-top shape is 25 beats every 30 seconds, but cyclist Miguel Indurain of Spain has the lowest ever resting heart rate at just 14 beats every 30 seconds.

1 SECOND

Not only can hummingbirds beat their wings 80 times a second, but their hearts also go at a speedy pace. Beating 21 times per second in flight, the hummingbird flies off with the record for fastest heartbeat on earth.

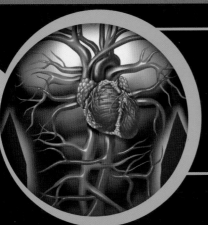

11 SECONDS

An adult human heart pumps 1 litre of blood every 11 seconds. It takes just one minute for all of a person's blood to go right around the body.

45 SECONDS

Black bears hibernate, or go to sleep for the winter without waking up for food or water. To save energy they slow their bodies down: The heart beats only six times in 45 seconds and the bear takes only one breath.

30 SECONDS

By reducing their heart rate to one beat every 30 seconds, the saltwater crocodiles of Australia and Asia can lurk underwater for two hours at a time. Don't try holding your breath that long unless you're part croc!

True or false

You can tell whether a pregnant woman is having a boy or girl by measuring the unborn baby's heart rate. If it's above 3 beats per second (bps), it's a girl. Below 3 bps (bps) means it's a boy.

(Answer on page 32)

The heart of a blue whale (the biggest mammal on Earth) weighs almost a tonne and pumps 270 litres of blood every second. This giant heart takes a beat every three seconds.

SECONDS 3

SECOND 1

The Cray Titan supercomputer in California, USA, is the fastest in the world. It can do 17.59 thousand trillion calculations per second. That's a lot of maths problems!

In 2011 Japanese ping pong aces Mima Ito and Tacshow Arai hit the ball back and forth over the net 90 times in just 30 seconds. That is three hits every second.

SECONDS 30

In China, 5,000 chopsticks are made every two seconds – and one whole tree is used in the process.

SECONDS 2

Millions of hot dogs are consumed every day in America. Each summer in the US, 818 hot dogs are eaten every second.

1 SECOND

SECONDS 0.003

The mantis shrimp uses its record-breaking punch to crack open crab shells. This little boxer jabs out its front legs in just three thousandths of a second. That is enough to pack a punch that has the speed and power of a bullet!

HOT DOG!

60

SECONDS 30

The 2012 Fourth of July celebrations in San Diego, Califonia, USA, went off with a bang. A mistake set off all the fireworks for the Big Bay Boom display in just over 30 seconds!

When a driver comes into the pits – the garage area beside the track in a Formula 1 Grand Prix – his team of mechanics must work fast. A pitstop is used to replace worn-out tyres – fresh ones help the car go even faster. In 2012 the McLaren F1 team's pit crew changed four tyres in an incredible 2.31 seconds!

SECONDS   2.31

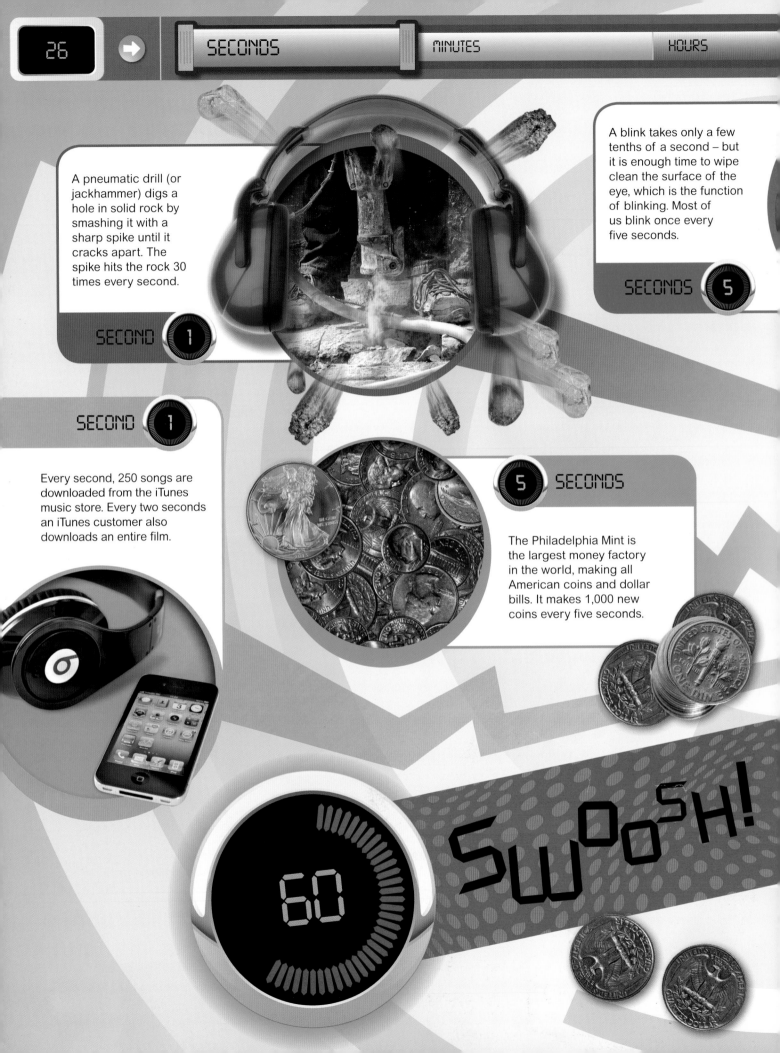

A pneumatic drill (or jackhammer) digs a hole in solid rock by smashing it with a sharp spike until it cracks apart. The spike hits the rock 30 times every second.

SECOND 1

SECOND 1

Every second, 250 songs are downloaded from the iTunes music store. Every two seconds an iTunes customer also downloads an entire film.

A blink takes only a few tenths of a second – but it is enough time to wipe clean the surface of the eye, which is the function of blinking. Most of us blink once every five seconds.

SECONDS 5

5 SECONDS

The Philadelphia Mint is the largest money factory in the world, making all American coins and dollar bills. It makes 1,000 new coins every five seconds.

60

SWOOSH!

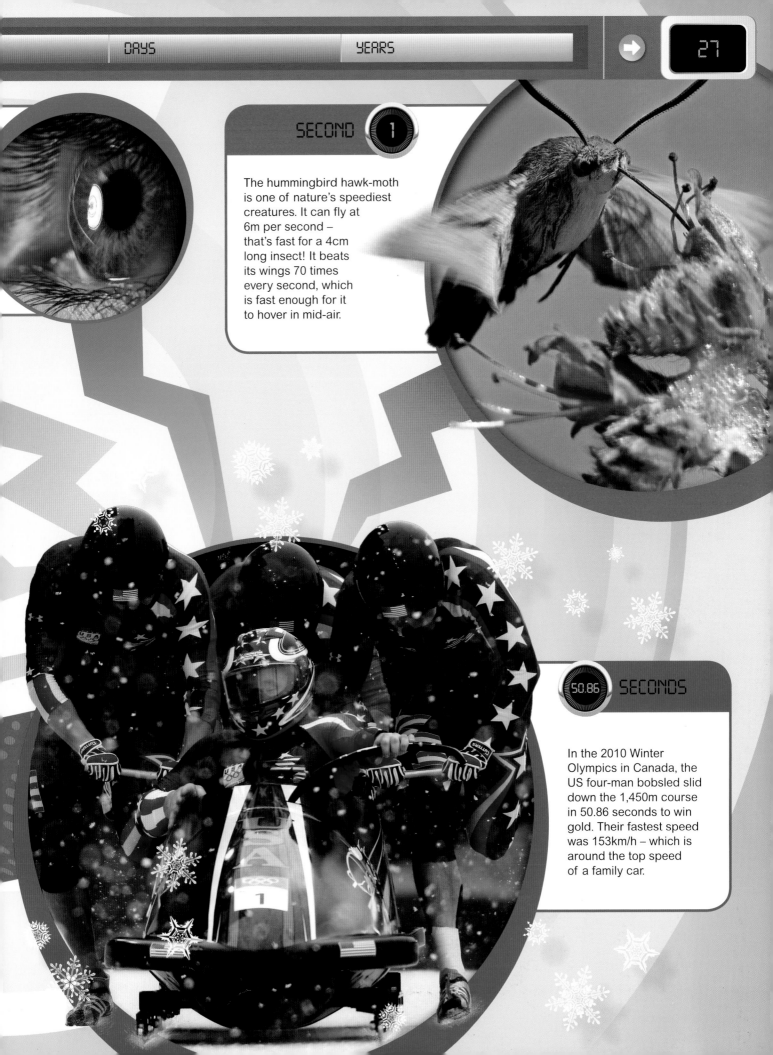

SECOND 1

The hummingbird hawk-moth is one of nature's speediest creatures. It can fly at 6m per second – that's fast for a 4cm long insect! It beats its wings 70 times every second, which is fast enough for it to hover in mid-air.

50.86 SECONDS

In the 2010 Winter Olympics in Canada, the US four-man bobsled slid down the 1,450m course in 50.86 seconds to win gold. Their fastest speed was 153km/h – which is around the top speed of a family car.

SECONDS   MINUTES   HOURS

5 SECONDS

Somewhere in Europe, three brand new washing machines are being bought every five seconds.

SUPPLY AND DEMAND

Every second products are whizzing through factories and into the shops. Find out how quickly we make common items – and how quickly we rush out of the shops with them.

Around 32 new car tyres are produced every second. That is enough to change 19 million flat tyres every week.

SECOND **1**

1 SECOND

Every second, 11 tonnes (that's 2.2 million sheets) of paper roll out of paper mills – made either from freshly cut trees or from recycling old pieces of paper.

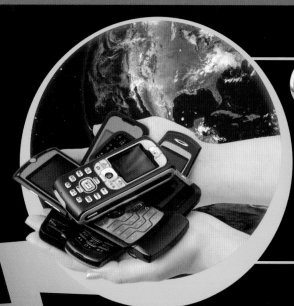

2 SECONDS

Every two seconds 100 mobile phone handsets are produced around the world. In some countries there are more mobile phones than there are people to talk into them.

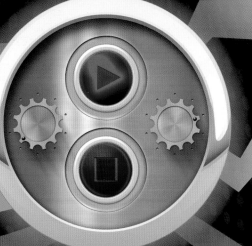

The world makes 2,940 sticks of gum a second. Gum loses its taste only because your tastebuds get tired and stop picking up the flavour!

SECOND 1

True or false
The largest producer of biros is French company Bic. Every five seconds they produce about 300 pens – enough for ten school classes.

(Answer on page 32)

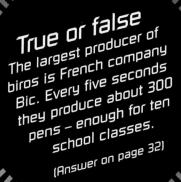

Every ten seconds, 780 pairs of feet put on a new pair of trainers. That's the same as everyone in Spain getting new shoes once a month.

10 SECONDS

1 SECOND

The fastest tap dancer of all is Irishman James Devine, who can tap his feet 38 times in a second!

SECOND 1

Pulsars are very small, but very heavy stars that spin around fast. PSR J1748-2446ad spins around 716 times every second. Planet Earth turns completely around only once a day!

In 2012 a group of 890 students broke a world record for the most pancakes flipped in 30 seconds. That's a big breakfast!

SECONDS 30

SPLASH!

60

 3.2 SECONDS

In 1987 Olivier Favre attempted to break the world record for highest dive from 53.9m above Villers-le-Lac in France. It took him 3.2 seconds to reach the water. The average high dive from 10m up takes just 1.4 seconds.

 10 SECONDS

Blind people read using a special alphabet called Braille. Braille shows each letter as a pattern of tiny dots poking out of the paper. The average reader can read about 21 words in just ten seconds using their fingertips.

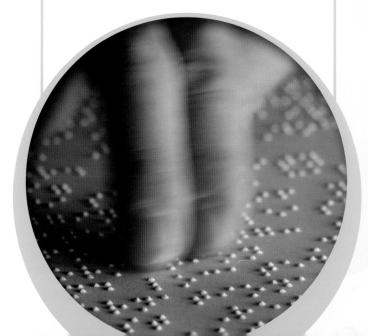

Every second, 15 million tonnes of water hit the Earth's surface, falling as drops from many thousands of rain showers happening at the same time around the world. That's enough to fill 93 million bath tubs!

SECOND 1

QUESTION 1

How many notes per second can the world's fastest violinist play?

A: 97
B: 15
C: 2

QUESTION 2

How many seconds will it take to travel up the Shanghai Tower in the world's fastest elevator?

A: 35
B: 135
C: 90

QUESTION 3

How many lightning strikes hit Earth's surface in ten seconds?

A: 450 B: 21 C: 45

QUIZ

60

QUESTION 4

How many hot dogs are eaten by Americans every second during the summer?

A: 6,545 B: 23 C: 818

TRUE OR FALSE

Page 13: FALSE – Google's Blogger publishes only 100,000 new words in 22 seconds. It takes 3.67 minutes to publish one million words.

Page 21: FALSE – There is no difference between the heart rate of an unborn boy and the heart rate of an unborn girl.

Page 29: TRUE

QUESTION 5

How long does it take for a nerve to carry a signal from your big toe to your brain?

A: 3 SECONDS
B: 0.02 SECONDS
C: 0.5 SECONDS

QUESTION 6

How long does it take to make 100 mobile phones?

A: 23 SECONDS
B: 2 SECONDS
C: 10 SECONDS

QUESTION 7

How long does it take for a drop of water to plunge all the way down the Angel Falls, the highest waterfall in the world?

A: 14 SECONDS
B: 32 SECONDS
C: 0.3 SECONDS

Answers 1: B 15, 2: A 35 seconds, 3: A 450, 4: C 818, 5: B 0.02 seconds, 6: B 2 seconds, 7: A 14 seconds

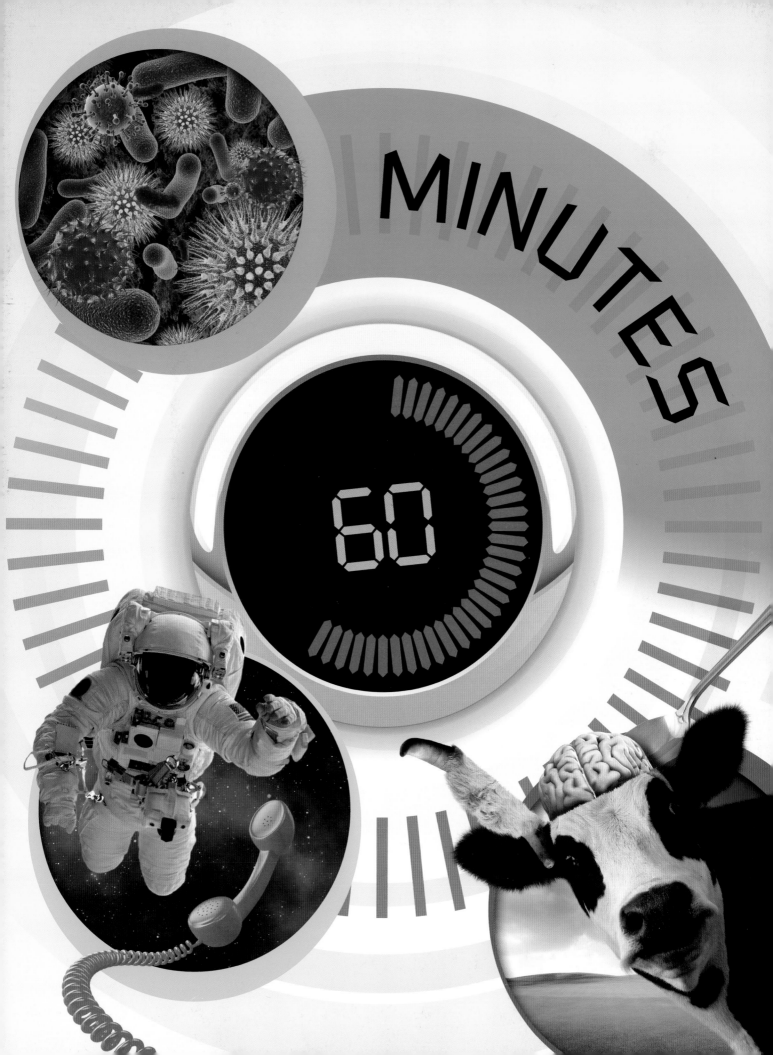

MINUTES

60

The Beatles were the biggest pop stars in history – and they are still going strong. The group has sold about 87 albums every minute of the last 50 years!

MINUTE 1

MINUTES 30

At 165m, the Singapore Flyer is the tallest ferris wheel in the world. It takes 30 minutes to go around once. Staying on for five spins is like flying from Berlin to Madrid.

MINUTES 4

In a solar eclipse, the Moon gets between the Sun and Earth and casts a huge shadow on us. Most eclipses last for just four minutes – then the Sun comes out, lighting up the world once more.

Cutting the woolly fleece off a sheep is called shearing. Using electric clippers, the best shearers can do 20 sheep in just 16 minutes. That's enough wool for 60 cosy jumpers.

 16 MINUTES

BAAA

60

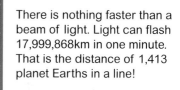

There is nothing faster than a beam of light. Light can flash 17,999,868km in one minute. That is the distance of 1,413 planet Earths in a line!

MINUTE 1

6 MINUTES

The average wind blows about 275m in a minute. Such a wind would take about six minutes to blow a nasty whiff across the Brooklyn Bridge!

Bagger 288 is a 200m-long monster digger and the largest wheeled vehicle in the world. It is also the fastest digger around. In 15 minutes its giant spinning shovels can dig a hole big enough for an Olympic-sized swimming pool.

15 MINUTES

Z'Z'Z'Z...

60

MINUTES 12

The fastest car allowed on ordinary roads (racing cars are banned) is the Bugatti Veyron. Its top speed is 431km/h, and that uses a lot of fuel. The Veyron can go at top speed for just 12 minutes before its tank runs dry.

1 MINUTE

Tsunamis are the world's fastest waves. Out at sea they can cover 12km in just a single minute. If they don't hit land, the waves can travel around the world in three days.

In 2009 American Richard Fink took a deep breath and held a note for 1.71 minutes – the longest ever recorded.

MINUTES **1.71**

10 MINUTES

It takes a long time for a lanky giraffe to lie down. Even so, giraffes sleep only for about ten minutes before it is time to get up again.

Thaneswar Guragai of Nepal is the fastest dribbler in the world – dribbling a basketball that is. In 2010 Thaneswar managed to bounce a ball 444 times in one minute.

1 MINUTE

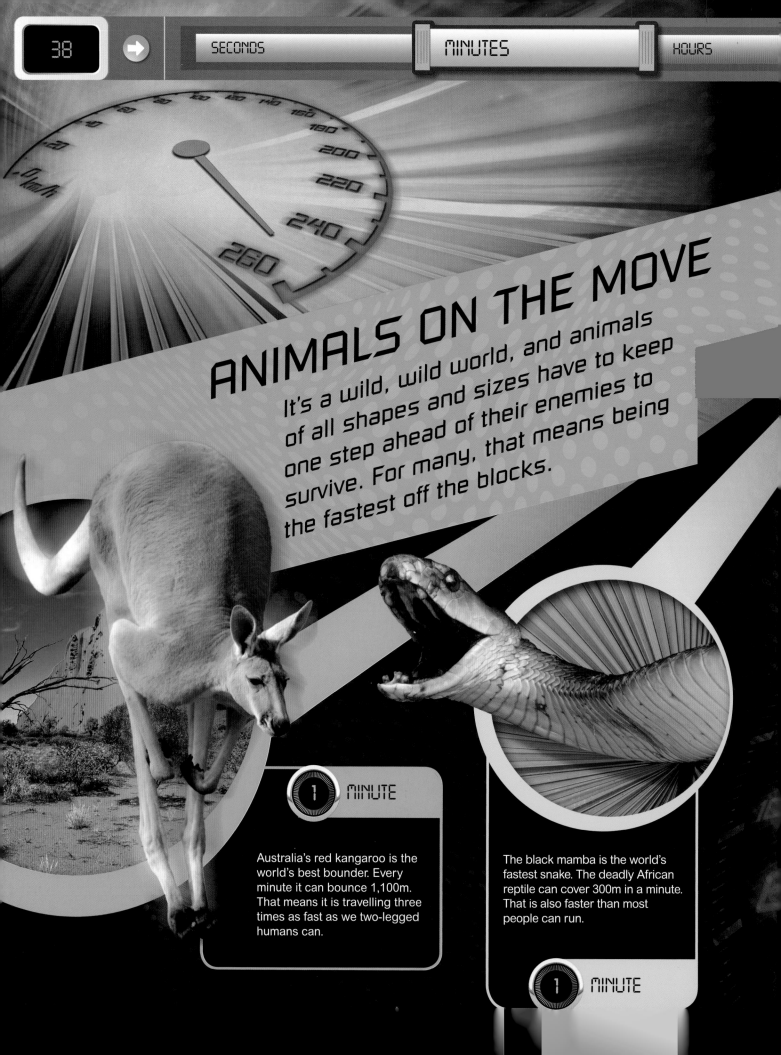

ANIMALS ON THE MOVE

It's a wild, wild world, and animals of all shapes and sizes have to keep one step ahead of their enemies to survive. For many, that means being the fastest off the blocks.

1 MINUTE

Australia's red kangaroo is the world's best bounder. Every minute it can bounce 1,100m. That means it is travelling three times as fast as we two-legged humans can.

1 MINUTE

The black mamba is the world's fastest snake. The deadly African reptile can cover 300m in a minute. That is also faster than most people can run.

1 MINUTE

The slow loris does not like attention and so creeps around very slowly. But it can speed up when it needs to – and run 800m per minute. That is faster than an Olympic sprinter (and it does it up a tree)!

1 MINUTE

The sailfish is the fastest animal in the sea. Its top speed is 109km/h, which means it covers 1,700m every minute. There are few speed boats around that can outrun this fish.

MINUTE 1

Although some birds go faster in steep swooping dives, the white-throated needletail flies fastest in a straight line. It covers 2,833m in a minute – faster than traffic moves along the motorway.

True or false

An adult mayfly does not feed and may live for only 30 minutes.

(Answer on see page 64)

The cheetah accelerates faster than most sports cars. It reaches a top speed of 113km/h in three seconds and can sprint 1,900m in one minute.

MINUTE 1

Most people are sound asleep just seven minutes after they put their head on the pillow. Sweet dreams!

MINUTES 7

ZZZZZZZZZZZZZ

ZZZZZZZZZZ

GaSP!

In 2012 Tom Sietas held his breath for 22 minutes (plus an extra 22 seconds) – smashing the world record. Don't try this at home, it's very dangerous! A doctor was on standby to help him if needed.

 22.37 MINUTES

 1 MINUTE

The British love a cup of tea. They use 130,000 tonnes of dried tea every year. To keep up the supply, the leaves of 989 tea bushes have to be picked every single minute.

20 MINUTES

One bacterium splits into two new 'daughters' every 20 minutes. A single germ can multiply into 69 billion bacteria in just 12 hours!

60

MINUTES 29

In 1984 Vicki Nelson and Jean Hepner, two American pro tennis players, whacked through the longest rally ever. They exchanged 643 shots in 29 minutes until Nelson finally won the point.

MINUTES 20

Louis-Antoine I became King of France on 2 August 1830. However, just 20 minutes later he was forced to abdicate (give up the throne), making him the shortest-reigning monarch in history.

4.32 MINUTES

In 2012 Austrian daredevil Felix Baumgartner flew to a height of 38,969m in a helium balloon as tall as ten houses. Felix wore a spacesuit just like an astronaut. But unlike an astronaut, Felix opened his capsule and jumped out. He fell for four minutes and 19 seconds. On the way down he broke the sound barrier, moving faster than sound at a speed of 1,357.6km/h – making him the fastest man ever.

60

CRASH!

Garden snails have only one foot so they wriggle along slowly. It takes a snail one minute to travel just 78cm – about the length of four pencils!

MINUTE **1**

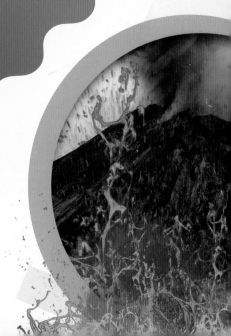

8 MINUTES

It takes eight minutes for light from the Sun to reach Earth. So if the Sun went out we wouldn't notice anything for a bit – and then it would get very dark (and cold).

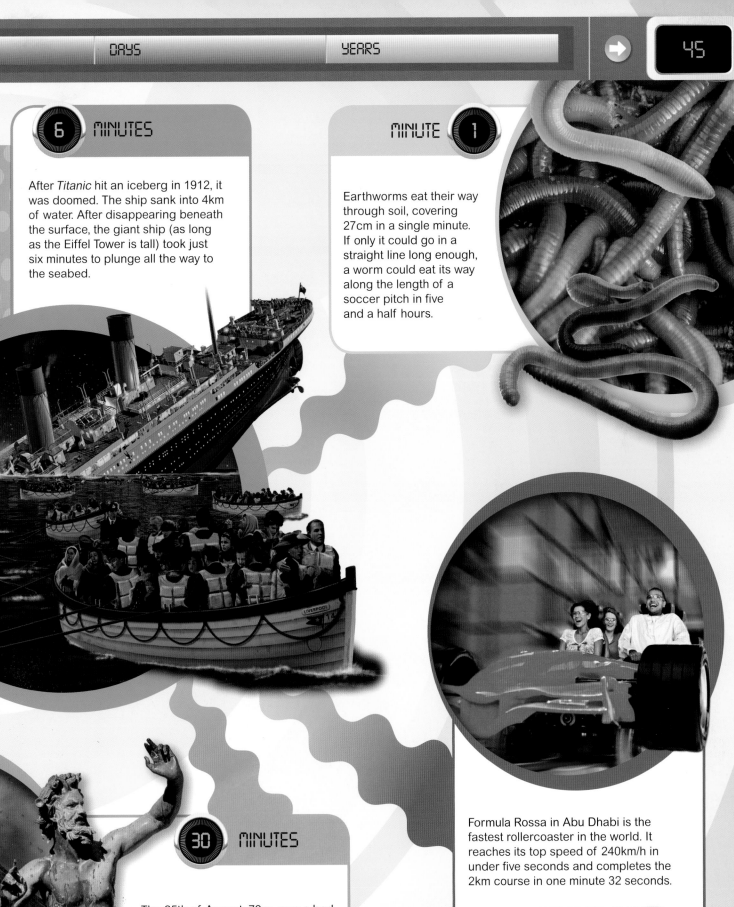

6 MINUTES

After *Titanic* hit an iceberg in 1912, it was doomed. The ship sank into 4km of water. After disappearing beneath the surface, the giant ship (as long as the Eiffel Tower is tall) took just six minutes to plunge all the way to the seabed.

MINUTE 1

Earthworms eat their way through soil, covering 27cm in a single minute. If only it could go in a straight line long enough, a worm could eat its way along the length of a soccer pitch in five and a half hours.

30 MINUTES

The 25th of August, 79CE, was a bad day for Pompeii, in Italy. Nearby, Mount Vesuvius released waves of hot ash. In just 30 minutes, the entire city was buried.

Formula Rossa in Abu Dhabi is the fastest rollercoaster in the world. It reaches its top speed of 240km/h in under five seconds and completes the 2km course in one minute 32 seconds.

MINUTES 1.5

Ken Edwards from England holds the record for eating live cockroaches. In 2001 he ate 36 cockroaches in one minute. That's a record that won't be beaten quickly!

MINUTE 1

 1 MINUTE

The British love potato crisps. They chomp through 11,400 packets every minute, making them the biggest crisp eaters in Europe.

COOKING TIME

Everyone's got to eat – and if you are lucky you get three meals a day. That adds up to 21 billion meal times across the world every day. Here are some of the wackiest meals you'll ever see.

 1 MINUTE

The Jagannath Temple in Puri, India, offers a meal to everyone who visits – and uses the world's largest kitchen with 250 ovens to do it. During festivals, the kitchen produces 139 meals every minute.

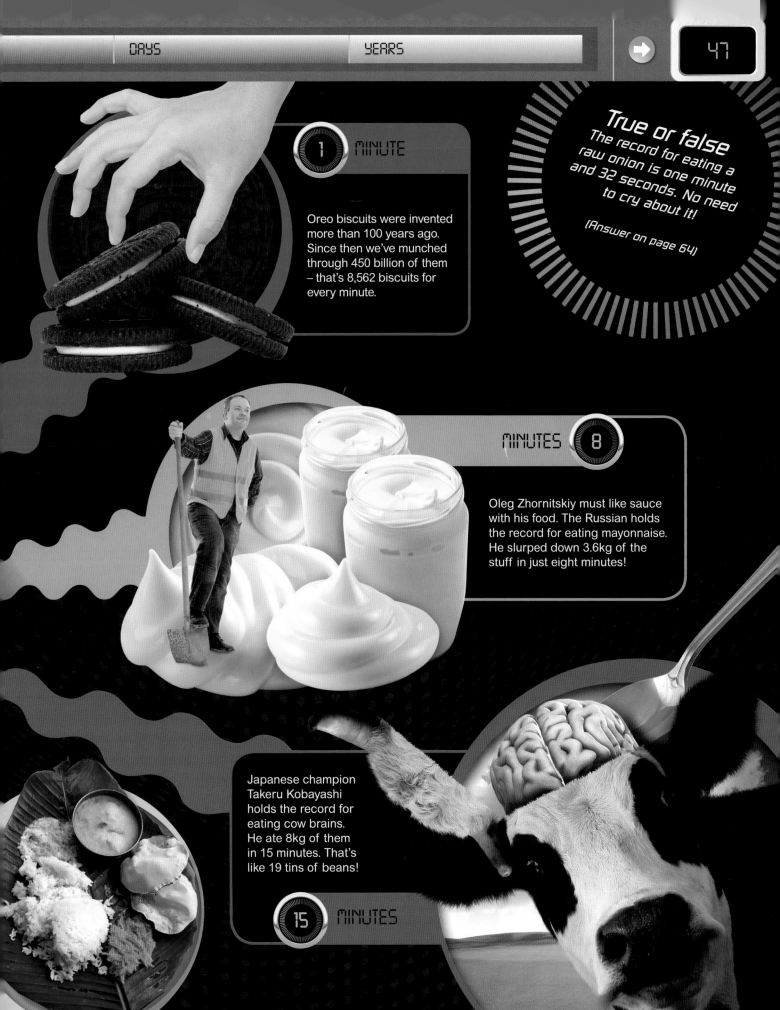

1 MINUTE

Oreo biscuits were invented more than 100 years ago. Since then we've munched through 450 billion of them – that's 8,562 biscuits for every minute.

True or false
The record for eating a raw onion is one minute and 32 seconds. No need to cry about it!

(Answer on page 64)

MINUTES 8

Oleg Zhornitskiy must like sauce with his food. The Russian holds the record for eating mayonnaise. He slurped down 3.6kg of the stuff in just eight minutes!

Japanese champion Takeru Kobayashi holds the record for eating cow brains. He ate 8kg of them in 15 minutes. That's like 19 tins of beans!

15 MINUTES

MINUTE 1

One million plastic bags are loaded with shopping every minute of every day.

MINUTES 6

SpaceShipTwo will be the first passenger spacecraft. The rocket plane flies higher than 100km, past the edge of space – but it stays there for only six minutes. That's still enough time to float around the cabin and enjoy the view.

MINUTES 10

Rainforests are so thick that a raindrop hitting the treetops will take ten minutes to splish and splash down to the ground.

Having a chat with an astronaut on Mars will be a lengthy business. It will take about 13 minutes for your voice signal to reach the red planet – and then another 13 for a reply to get back to you on Earth.

26 MINUTES

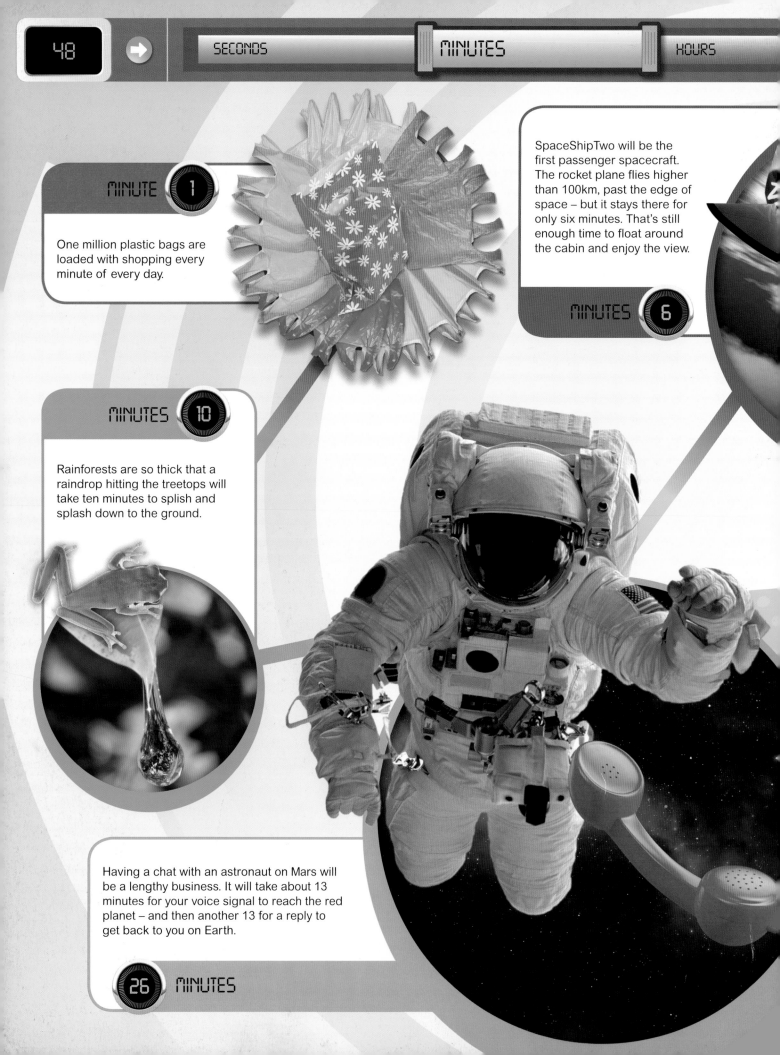

MINUTES 38

At 9:02am on 27 August 1896 Britain and Zanzibar went to war. The war ended at 9:40am when Zanzibar surrendered, making the 38-minute Anglo-Zanzibar War the shortest in history.

HELP?

60

Venera 7 was the first space probe to land on another planet. It touched down on Venus in 1970. However, the planet is so hot (twice as hot as a kitchen oven) that the spacecraft broke down after just 23 minutes.

MINUTES 23

MINUTE 1

Every minute 115 footballs are kicked out by factories around the world. That is almost enough for playing all the matches in two World Cup tournaments.

YUMMY!

60

The human body makes 144 million red blood cells every minute – to replace the ones that die. The red colour from the dead cells becomes a brown substance that colours your poo!

MINUTE 1

 **15 MINUTES**

Moles dig through soft soil at a top speed of 1m every 15 minutes, all thanks to their wide, spade-shaped front legs.

The first cars were known as horseless carriages. The 1892 Benz Viktoria took one minute to travel 300m. But a horse-drawn carriage could go three times as far in that time.

MINUTE 1

An anteater slurps up 30,000 ants a day. Each ant is captured with a lick of its long tongue. It's as long as your arm, but even so that tongue flickers in and out 160 times a minute.

MINUTE  1

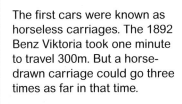

18 MINUTES

The SR-71 Blackbird is the fastest piloted aircraft ever built. In 1976 it flew 1,000km (the distance from Miami to Atlanta) in just under 18 minutes. That is an average speed of 3,367.22km/h, which is almost three times faster than sound!

MINUTES 8

The Shuttle was the first spaceplane. The journey to its orbit – the path it followed around Earth about 300km above the surface – took just eight minutes.

GOING FASTER

How fast is fast? Time to find out! Explore the speediest vehicles ever invented.

1 MINUTE

Thrust SSC is the only supersonic car. It is powered by a jet engine and, at full speed, the car travels 20km in just under a minute. That's twice the speed of the world's fastest train.

True or false

The Wright Flyer was the first aeroplane with an engine. Its maiden flight in 1903, with Orville Wright at the controls, lasted only 12 minutes.

(Answer on page 64)

26 MINUTES

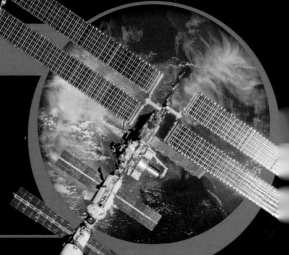

The International Space Station moves along at 27,724km/h and flies across the Pacific Ocean in just 26 minutes. A passenger jet would take more than 14 hours!

1.5 MINUTES

Superbikes have a bigger engine than many cars. With a top speed of about 300km/h, the best riders complete a racing lap every 1.5 minutes.

The PlanetSolar yacht has no sails to catch the wind. It has solar panels covering the area of almost two tennis courts. They harness enough solar energy to drive the boat 1km in just over two minutes.

MINUTES 2

Every hour or so the Old Faithful geyser in Yellowstone National Park in the USA spouts out enough water to fill 100 baths. The watery show can last up to five minutes.

MINUTES 5

On its first day of sale, 7,659 copies of *Harry Potter and the Deathly Hallows* were sold every single minute.

1 MINUTE

9 MINUTES

Yves 'Jetman' Rossy has carbon-fibre wings fitted with four tiny jets. His longest flight so far was across the English Channel in 2008. He did it in just over nine minutes. The ferry takes 90 minutes.

MINUTES **33**

The tide comes up some rivers so fast it forms a wave called a bore. Brazilian Serginho Laus was the first person to surf more than 10km on a bore, riding the wave of the Araguari River for just over 33 minutes.

A big swarm of locusts contains 40 billion insects! That crowd can eat 56 tonnes of food – or a wheat field the size of seven football pitches – every minute.

 MINUTE **1**

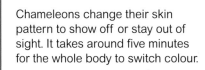

Chameleons change their skin pattern to show off or stay out of sight. It takes around five minutes for the whole body to switch colour.

5 MINUTES

BLAST!

 **60**

1 MINUTE

People say: 'There's one born every minute!' In fact there are 251 babies born every minute, all around the world. More than a billion children have been born in the last ten years alone! Were you one of them?

In 1987 James Carvill from Northern Ireland played 18 holes of golf in a record time of just over 27 minutes. In 2008 a team of 40 American golfers playing in relay, completed 18 holes in just under eight minutes!

MINUTES **27**

60

PoP!

It is estimated that a grown-up laughs once every 84 minutes. Children laugh a lot more. The average five-year-old laughs every ten minutes.

10 MINUTES

Popcorn is the only food that explodes before it is ready to eat. Every minute we pop one tonne of the snack – the weight of half a hippo!

MINUTE **1**

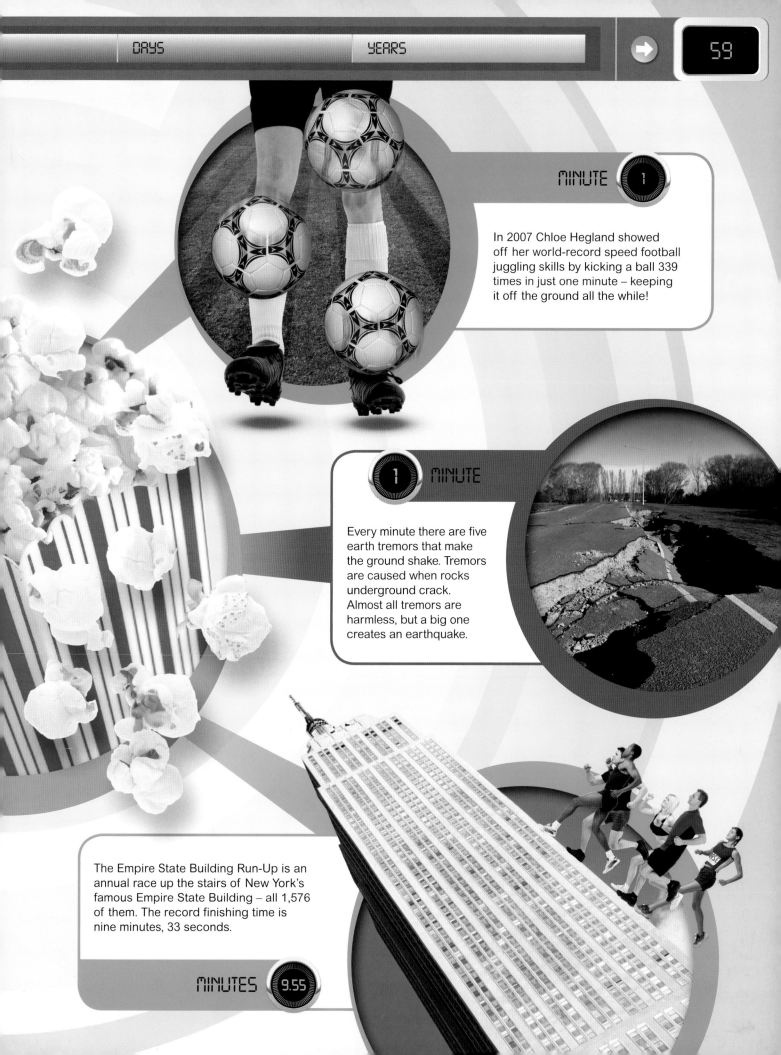

MINUTE 1

In 2007 Chloe Hegland showed off her world-record speed football juggling skills by kicking a ball 339 times in just one minute – keeping it off the ground all the while!

1 MINUTE

Every minute there are five earth tremors that make the ground shake. Tremors are caused when rocks underground crack. Almost all tremors are harmless, but a big one creates an earthquake.

The Empire State Building Run-Up is an annual race up the stairs of New York's famous Empire State Building – all 1,576 of them. The record finishing time is nine minutes, 33 seconds.

MINUTES 9.55

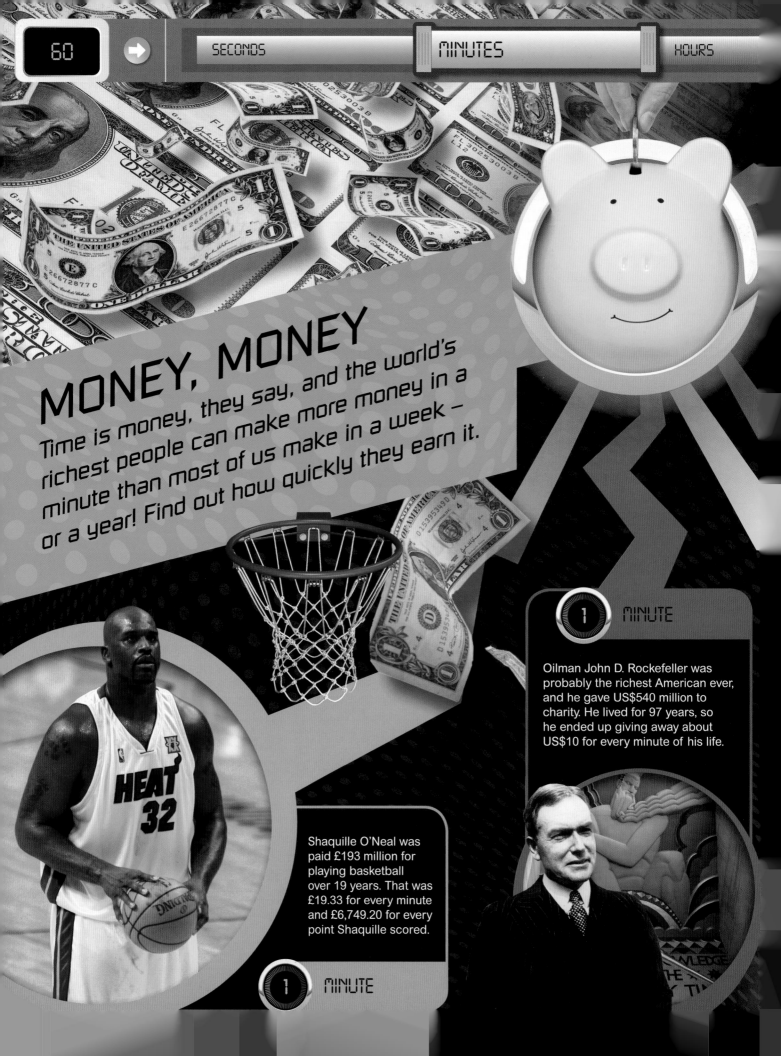

MONEY, MONEY

Time is money, they say, and the world's richest people can make more money in a minute than most of us make in a week – or a year! Find out how quickly they earn it.

1 MINUTE

Oilman John D. Rockefeller was probably the richest American ever, and he gave US$540 million to charity. He lived for 97 years, so he ended up giving away about US$10 for every minute of his life.

Shaquille O'Neal was paid £193 million for playing basketball over 19 years. That was £19.33 for every minute and £6,749.20 for every point Shaquille scored.

1 MINUTE

1 MINUTE

Tom Cruise was paid £62,000 for every minute of *Mission: Impossible – Ghost Protocol*, one of his most popular films. It lasted 133 minutes earning him a total of £8,246,000!

1 MINUTE

Lionel Messi is the highest-paid football star. In 2012 he was paid £27.5m for 67 matches (and scoring 91 goals). That is £4,560 for every minute on the pitch.

French cosmetics billionaire Liliane Bettencourt is the richest woman in the world. She has had a good few years. In 2009 her fortune was US$13.4 billion; today it is US$30 billion – a rise of $6,317 every minute for the last five years.

1 MINUTE

In 1947 Italian baker Michelle Ferrero invented the nut and chocolate recipe for Ferrero Rocher. In 2012 Michelle's chocs earned his company £6.6 billion – or a tasty £100,000 every eight minutes.

8 MINUTES

1 MINUTE

The solar wind is a stream of super-hot particles. In one minute it travels an amazing 24,000km! That is the distance from Sydney to Abu Dhabi and back. The wind hits Earth around the poles and creates the Northern or Southern Lights.

In 2008 Ben Pridmore from England took ten minutes to remember the exact order of seven packs of playing cards. That's a total of 364 cards (seriously, no jokers allowed)!

MINUTES 10

MINUTES 4.03

In 2010 New Zealander Dave Mullins swam 265m underwater, holding his breath for four minutes and two seconds. That is like swimming just over ten lengths of a normal public swimming pool.

SPIN!

60

1 MINUTE

A gyrator spin is when the rider of a BMX balances on one wheel and spins around. In 2011 Japanese rider Takahiro Ikeda showed how it was done by doing 59 gyrator spins in just one minute – the current world record.

3.43 MINUTES

The biggest recorded flash mob was in April 2012, when 50,000 people suddenly started dancing across America. It lasted for three minutes and 26 seconds – then everything went back to normal.

Which animal has the deadliest venom? A snake? A scorpion? How about a snail! The geographic cone snail spears small fish with a harpoon-like tongue. The venom in a jab is enough to kill a human in just five minutes.

MINUTES 5

QUESTION 1

How quickly can the best sheep shearers cut the wool from 20 sheep?

A: 30 MINUTES
B: 5.5 MINUTES
C: 16 MINUTES

QUESTION 2

How far can a black mamba slither in a minute?

A: 50 M
B: 300 M
C: 1K M

QUESTION 3

How long does it take the average person to drop off to sleep?

A: 7 MINUTES
B: 0.5 MINUTES
C: 23 MINUTES

QUESTION 4

What is the world record for eating live cockroaches?

A: 36 PER MINUTE
B: 0 PER MINUTE
C: 254 PER MINUTE

TRUE OR FALSE

Page 39: TRUE
Page 47: TRUE
Page 53: FALSE – The Wright Flyer's first flight lasted 12 seconds and covered a distance of 37m. Later the same day, Orville's brother Wilbur made a flight lasting 59 seconds.

60 QUIZ

QUESTION 5

How long did it take for Yves Rossy to fly across the English Channel with his jet-powered wingpack?

A: 2.3 MINUTES
B: 45 MINUTES
C: 9 MINUTES

QUESTION 6

How many dollars did John D. Rockefeller give to charity for every minute of his life?

A: $2 MILLION
B: $2,902
C: $10

QUESTION 7

How quickly can a bite from a geographic cone snail kill a person?

A: 5 MINUTES
B: 25 MINUTES
C: 0.5 MINUTES

Answers 1: C 16 minutes, 2: B 300m, 3: A 7 minutes, 4: A 36 per minute, 5: C 9 minutes, 6: A $10, 7: A 5 minutes

HOURS

24

HOURS 6

In 2012 it took 150 Portuguese chefs six hours to cook a 10m omelette made from 145,000 eggs and half a tonne of oil and butter.

24

YAWN

16 **HOURS**

If you see a sloth at the zoo the chances are it will be fast asleep. Captive sloths sleep for up to 16 hours a day. Their wild cousins sleep for less than ten hours.

HOURS 10

Jupiter spins more than twice as fast as Earth, going round once every ten hours. (Earth takes 24 hours to rotate.)

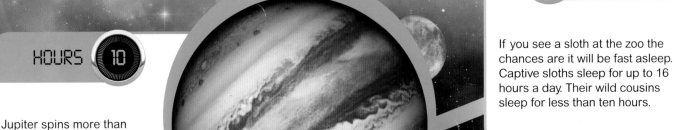

A game of American football lasts one hour and is measured on the game clock. That runs only when the ball is in play so a one-hour football game takes more than three hours from start to finish!

HOURS **3**

A glacier is a river of ice flowing downhill very slowly. One of the world's fastest glaciers is Jakobshavn Isbrae in Greenland, which whizzes along at 83cm every hour – that's nearly the length of a guitar.

HOUR **1**

The world's deserts are getting bigger. Every hour, an area of land equivalent to 52,615 tennis courts becomes desert.

HOUR **1**

VROOM!

The average person can read about 30 pages – or about 7,500 words – of a book in one hour. The world's fastest typists can write the same number in 40 minutes!

HOUR 1

 1 HOUR

Leaving a car engine running for an hour uses the same amount of petrol as driving 50km on a motorway.

4.5 HOURS

Apollo 17 astronauts did not just do the moonwalk – they also went for a moondrive. They clocked up 4.5 hours in the moon buggy – but travelled only 36km around their lander. That's like driving around Central Park just under four times.

Little brown bats always come out at night to catch flying insects to eat. They hunt for around five hours and catch 60,000 insects in that time.

HOURS 5

ROUTE 6

HOUR 1

In 1910 a group of 10,000 workers started building a 610km road from Davenport to Council Bluffs in Iowa, USA, at 9am. By 10am they had finished. But it took the rest of the day to get the road signs up! Even in today's cars it would take more than five hours to drive along the whole road.

MAP OF IOWA
Population 1,624,615
Area sq. miles 55,47

8 HOURS

The body produces about 25ml of sweat an hour. The sweat we produce during a night in bed would be enough to fill a small glass.

Humans produce eight teaspoons of saliva every hour. Luckily we swallow it all automatically, otherwise we'd make quite a mess!

HOUR 1

BODY FACTS

The body never turns off – it's working away around the clock. In fact it has its own timer called a circadian rhythm, which tells it when it is time to eat, sleep and wake up. Let's clock some body facts.

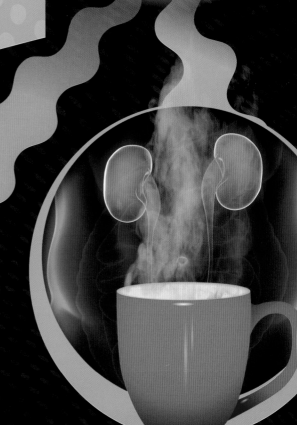

People don't all poo the same amount each day – it depends on how much we eat. However, on average, humans are producing 18 grams of poo every hour.

HOUR 1

True or false
People find it hard to concentrate for long. During a task that takes an hour, people spend a third of the time (20 minutes) daydreaming.

(Answer on page 96)

1 HOUR

In 1981 Donna Griffiths from England had a sneezing fit. She sneezed on average 114 times per hour – that's one million a year – for the next 978 days (2.5 years).

An adult human's kidneys produce 250ml of urine every four hours. That is enough to fill a steamy coffee mug.

HOURS 4

An adult sleeps for around eight hours a night. Ten-year-olds need about ten hours, while newborn babies sleep for about 18 hours – although not always at night!

HOURS 8

In 2012 cooks at the Black Bear Casino in Minnesota, USA, flipped the largest hamburger ever – it weighed a tonne! It took four hours to cook the patty and the 3m bun took seven hours to bake.

HOURS 4

HOURS 20

A modern car is made from 30,000 parts but it takes just 20 hours to put them all together. That's less than one day. Even then most of that time is taken up waiting for the paint to dry!

HOURS 20.25

The longest time on a pogo stick was 20 hours and 13 minutes, a record set by James Roumeliotis in California, USA in 2011. In that time he made 206,864 bounces.

People in the United States spend £3 million on pet food every two hours. That's enough for two million packets of dog biscuits.

2 HOURS

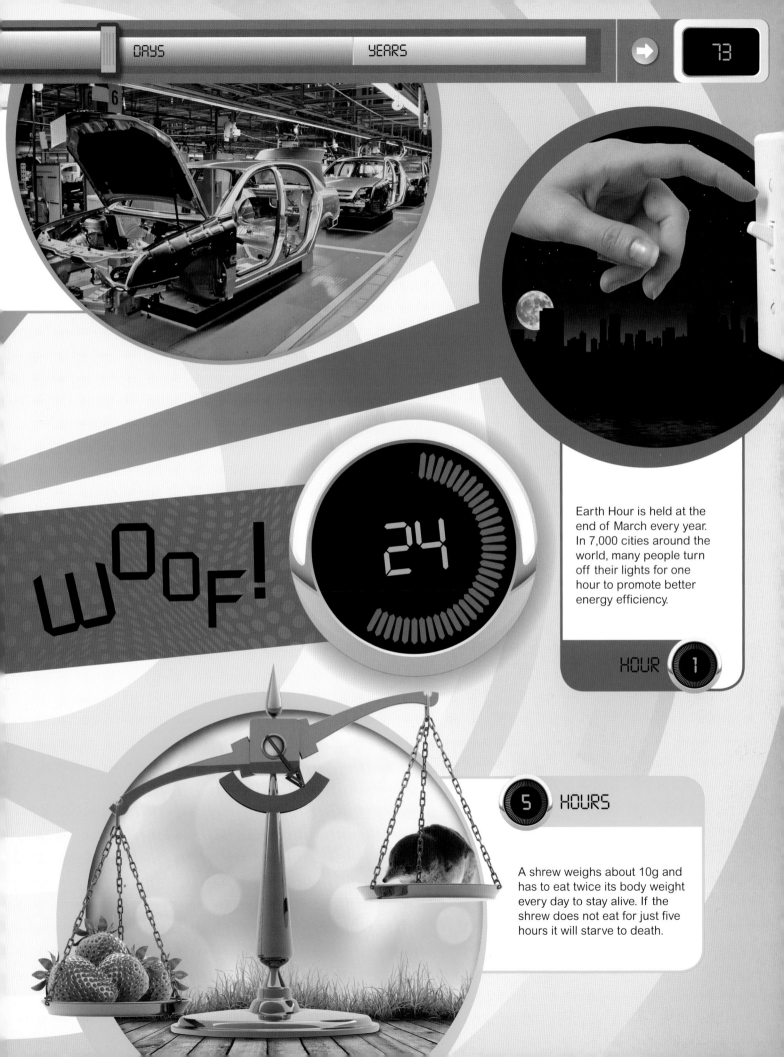

WOoF!

24

Earth Hour is held at the end of March every year. In 7,000 cities around the world, many people turn off their lights for one hour to promote better energy efficiency.

HOUR 1

5 HOURS

A shrew weighs about 10g and has to eat twice its body weight every day to stay alive. If the shrew does not eat for just five hours it will starve to death.

SECONDS MINUTES HOURS

HOURS 1.5

Sperm whales are the largest hunting mammals on Earth. They are also the deepest divers. These whales can swim deeper than 1km – like swimming to the bottom of the Grand Canyon – and stay down there for 1.5 hours at a time. They dive into the deep to do battle with their mysterious prey – giant squid!

HOURS

HOUR 1

Plankton is the name for small living things that float in the ocean. Most of it is too tiny to see without a microscope. Twenty-four million tonnes of plankton grows in the ocean every hour. That is the weight of about four million elephants.

SWIM!

In 2012 brother and sister Charley and George Phillips became the fastest woman and man to run a marathon on stilts. They crossed the line together, running the 42.19km race in six hours and 50 minutes. People running marathons without stilts take half the time.

HOURS 6.83

A standard DVD holds 133 minutes of film, stored as a code on the shiny side. A laser reads the code as the disc spins around. It takes 49,324 spins for all 2.22 hours of video to be decoded.

2.22 HOURS

Russian Yuri Gagarin was the first person to fly into space in 1961. He was up there for one hour and 8 seconds. For half of that time, mission control back on Earth had no idea if Yuri was alive or dead!

HOUR  1.1

The average American eats 46 slices of pizza a year. That means 32,000 pizzas are eaten in the US every hour! That's more than half of all the pizza in the world.

HOUR 1

HOUR 1

About 1,000 tonnes of coffee beans are picked every single hour. That's 6.9 billion beans, enough to fill 46 container lorries!

A sperm whale produces more than one tonne of poo every hour. However, it does not all go to waste. The poo contains a wax called ambergris, which is used in the best perfumes!

HOUR **1**

HOURS **2**

There are 19,000 pieces of space junk orbiting Earth and they all go around every two hours. Most are smaller than a chocolate bar but large enough to damage a spacecraft if they hit one.

WHAT A WASTE OF TIME!

We are surrounded by waste. But just how fast – and how much – is piling up on Earth as you read this? Waste no more time and find out.

1 HOUR

Humans use more than 26 million aluminium cans an hour. Recycling just one of those cans saves enough energy to power a TV for three hours.

Every hour people throw out 5,700 tonnes of electronic junk – the weight of 40 blue whales. That includes 3,400 computers and 16,000 mobile phones. The 'e-waste' is filled with toxic chemicals that must be cleaned up to prevent pollution.

1 HOUR

A cow releases about 12 litres of methane gas every hour. That's enough to blow up two party balloons. Some of the gas comes out in farts but most is burped out in bovine belches.

HOUR 1

12 HOURS

Americans produce a quarter of the world's waste. In just over 12 hours the average American throws away 1kg of garbage.

True or false
Nuclear waste gives out dangerous radiation. However, it becomes harmless after storing it for 18 hours.

(Answer on page 96)

In 2001 NASA astronauts Susan Helms and James Voss went for the longest spacewalk. They were outside for eight hours and 56 minutes upgrading the International Space Station.

 8.9 HOURS

The world's longest sandwich was made in three hours by 250 chefs in Dubai, UAE. It was 2,667m, about the length of the Golden Gate Bridge. It contained 600 jars of cream cheese, 525kg of tomatoes and 100kg of olives.

HOURS 3

 1 HOUR

There are no longer plenty more fish in the sea. In the 1970s, 39 tonnes of cod were caught every hour by fishing boats in the North Sea. Today the catch is just three tonnes – we have eaten a lot of fish!

 24

HUGE!

SANDWICH
ENDS
3KM

Our brain follows a sleep cycle that begins when we doze off and lasts around 1.5 hours. The last ten minutes of the cycle are when we dream. Then we normally wake for a few seconds before dropping off to sleep again.

HOURS 1.5

1 HOUR

The largest supertankers are like a floating Empire State Building. Ships this big take one hour to turn – moving in a circle that is 2.5km wide – and are big enough to contain 45 Roman Colosseums.

1 HOUR

Every hour the Twittersphere receives 16 million tweets. Each user is not allowed to post more than 40 messages per hour!

The longest-lasting tornado ever recorded was in 1925. It kept on spinning for 3.5 hours, starting in Ellington, Missouri, USA, and ending in Princeton, Indiana, 352km away. Most tornadoes last a few minutes.

HOURS 3.5

HOURS 4.75

In 1960 Jacques Piccard and Don Walsh took four hours and 47 minutes to become the first people to reach Challenger Deep. This is the deepest place on Earth's sea bed, 10,898m down. The water is so deep that if you sunk Mount Everest there its peak would still be 2,000m under the water.

Pemba Dorje Sherpa holds the record for the fastest climb up Mount Everest. In 2004 he reached the 8,848m summit eight hours and ten minutes after leaving Base Camp, 3,484m below. Most people take a couple of days.

HOURS 8.16

24

TwEET!

3 HOURS

Bracken Cave in Texas is home to 20 million bats – the biggest bat roost in the world. Every summer evening the bats fly out to hunt bugs. It takes three hours for all the bats to leave.

In 2009 David Slick from Texas, USA, juggled three balls non-stop for 12 hours and five minutes, setting a new world record.

HOURS 12.08

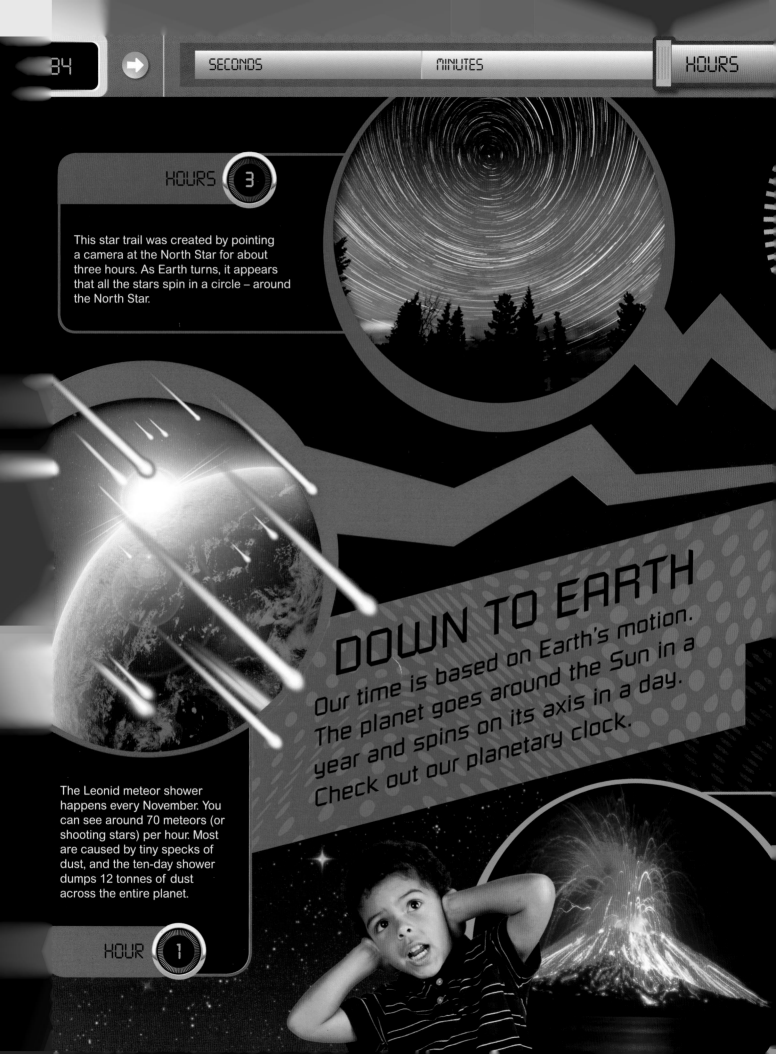

HOURS 3

This star trail was created by pointing a camera at the North Star for about three hours. As Earth turns, it appears that all the stars spin in a circle – around the North Star.

DOWN TO EARTH

Our time is based on Earth's motion. The planet goes around the Sun in a year and spins on its axis in a day. Check out our planetary clock.

The Leonid meteor shower happens every November. You can see around 70 meteors (or shooting stars) per hour. Most are caused by tiny specks of dust, and the ten-day shower dumps 12 tonnes of dust across the entire planet.

HOUR 1

True or false

Sound travels much faster through water than air. A loud whale song can travel right across the Atlantic Ocean in just under an hour.

(Answer on page 96)

1 HOUR

It takes 24 hours (or one day) for Earth to spin around completely – that is a turn of 360 degrees. So in one hour it turns 15 degrees. If you go west by 15 degrees, the time goes back one hour. If you go the same distance east, the time goes forward an hour.

1 HOUR

In one hour Earth moves 107,218km in its journey around the Sun (which takes all year). That is like flying from London to Tokyo and back five times.

2.5 HOURS

The speed of sound in Earth's atmosphere is 1,236 km/h. The loudest sound ever heard was the eruption of the Krakatoa volcano in 1883 in Indonesia. Two and a half hours later, the explosion was heard in Perth, Australia (3,110km away).

HOURS 4

There are eight planets in the Solar System. The furthest away is Neptune. The Sun's light takes four hours to reach this cold, icy planet. (It reaches Earth in just eight minutes!)

The Bingham Canyon copper mine in Utah, USA, is the largest hole ever dug. It could fit 500 Great Pyramids inside. It is getting bigger – every hour another 17,000 tonnes of rock is dug out.

HOUR 1

HOURS 1.5

There is only one swimming race where the start is in a different continent to the finish. Turkey's Swim Hellespont event starts in Asia, and competitors must cross 5km of water to reach Europe. If you don't finish in 1.5 hours, you're out!

Fidel Castro was the leader of Cuba. He was famous for giving the longest speeches of any world leader. His longest ever went on for seven hours and 10 minutes.

HOURS 7.16

Every August, the Tomatina, the largest food fight in the world, takes place in Buñeol, Spain. For exactly one hour, 40,000 people throw 150,000 squashed tomatoes (weighing a total of 40 tonnes) at each other.

HOUR 1

Frenchman Alain Robert is a real-life spiderman. In 2011 he took 6.25 hours climb 829.8m up Burj Khalifa, the fastest time for climbing the tallest building in the world.

HOURS 6.25

SPLAT!

24

HOURS 12

An albatross has the longest wingspan of any bird – around 3m from tip to tip. By catching the wind, the bird can cover about 500km in 12 hours without flapping its wings once. That's the distance from London to Edinburgh.

If all the world's Lego bricks were divided equally among the people of the world we would have 53 each. The Danish company makes 2,160,000 new bricks every hour!

HOUR 1

HOUR 1

The largest number of hot air balloons to take off in one hour is 345. This record was achieved in the USA at the Albuquerque International Balloon Fiesta in 2011.

FLOAT

Orb web spiders are common in gardens around the world. They weave a new web every night in autumn. It takes a spider about an hour to weave its spiral web.

1 HOUR

Big solar storms blast out 1.6 billion tonnes of hot gas – that is the mass of 3,000 skyscrapers – which takes about 13 hours to reach Earth. When the storms hit us, they can knock out power supplies for a little while.

13 HOURS

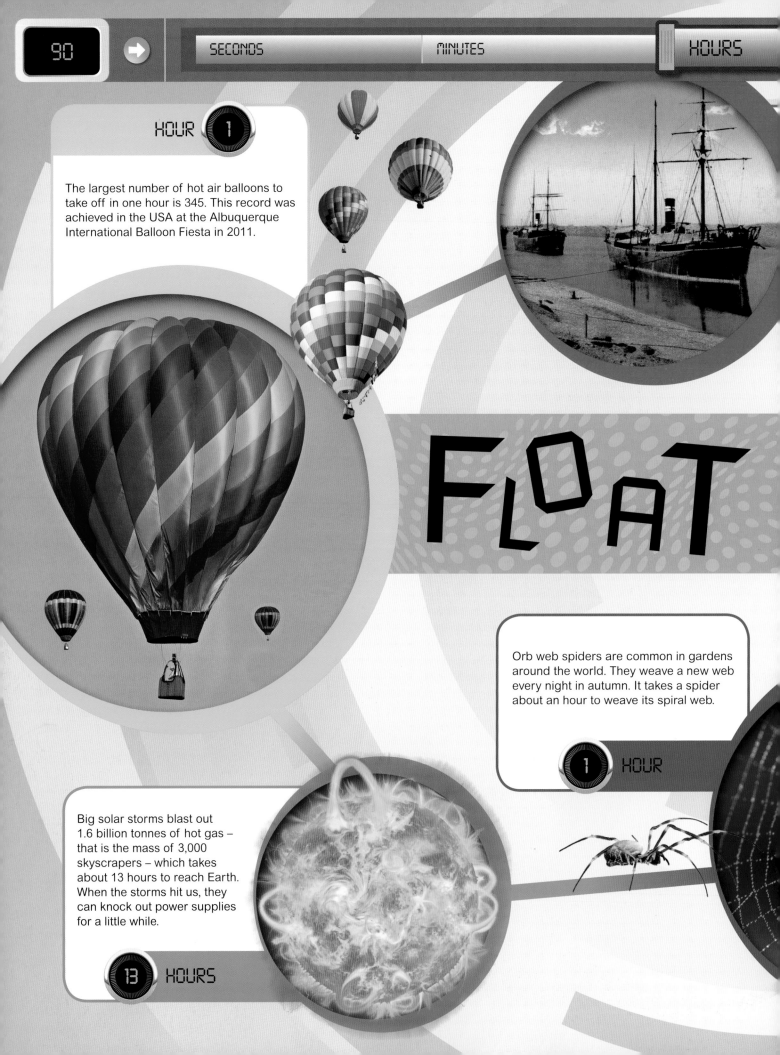

It takes 15 hours for a ship to travel through the Suez Canal. The 163km long canal was dug in the 1860s to connect the Red Sea to the Mediterranean.

HOURS **15**

24

It takes about 13 hours to hike from one side of the Grand Canyon to the other. It is just 7km straight across, but to get there you have to walk a total of 33km and climb down 1,767m to the bottom – and then back up the other side!

HOURS **13**

1.45 HOURS

In 2009 Boo Chan from Australia ran 10km while hulahooping in 1 hour 27 minutes – the fastest ever time by a woman.

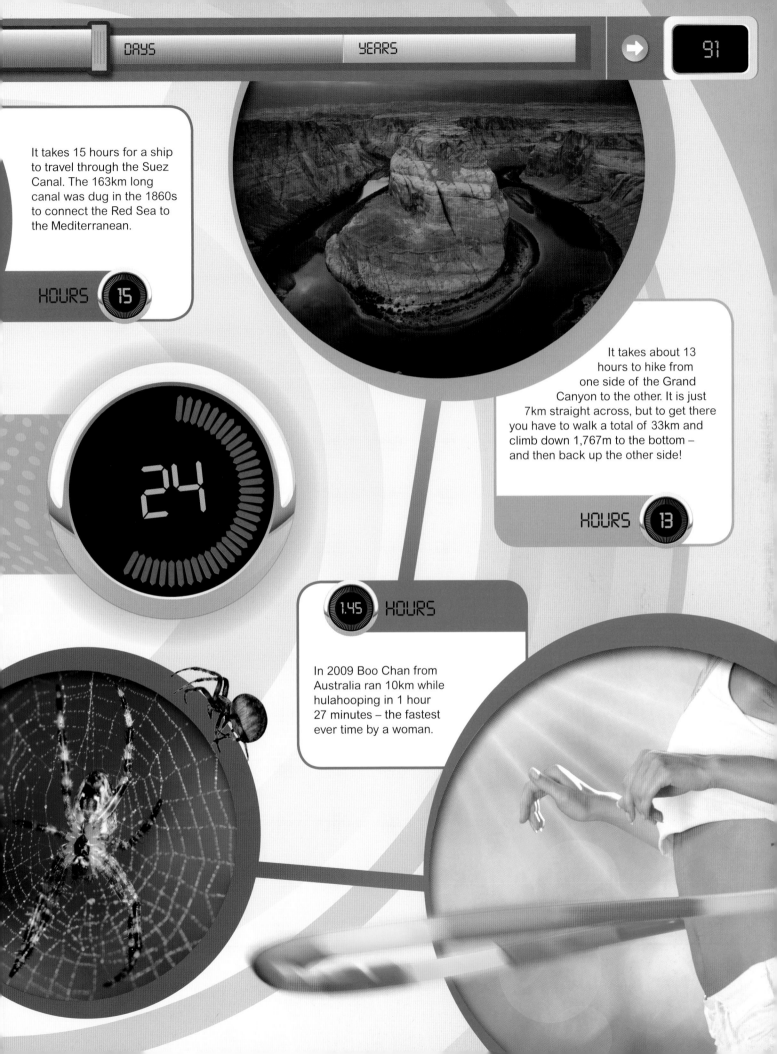

FUN TIMES

Take some time out! Play a game, surf the web or watch a film. It's time to be entertained.

4 HOURS

The four-hour opening ceremony of the 2008 Beijing Olympic Games in China had 984 million people tuning in at some point during the amazing show. That makes it the most watched TV show ever.

Every hour 3,874 games consoles were sold during 2012.

1 HOUR

6.6 HOURS

Forget Hollywood, the biggest movie producer is Bollywood, the film industry in Mumbai, India. A new film is completed every 6.6 hours, adding up to 1,325 a year.

7 HOURS

The ABC-Yahoo service is the biggest news web site on the Internet. Every seven hours, one million people will use it to check the news.

1 HOUR

There is no need to go to the cinema – we can send movies straight to our TVs. Every hour 388,127 films are being streamed into our homes.

TV fans in Thailand spend an average of 3.2 hours in front of the television every day. That makes them the biggest viewers in the world.

HOURS 3.2

True or false?
Sitting close to the television for more than an hour will damage your eyesight.

(Answer on page 96)

In the northern hemisphere the longest day of the year is normally 21 June. In Europe and the United States the Sun is up for more than 15 hours that day. (The shortest day is 21 December.)

HOURS 15

24

SWISH!

 5 HOURS

BigDog, a four-legged robot built for the US military, can walk for five hours and cross 20km of rough terrain – the length of Manhattan – before running out of fuel.

4 HOURS

The Vasaloppet in Sweden is the longest and biggest cross-country ski race in the world. Every year about 15,000 skiers compete to finish the 90km course, with the best skiers taking just under four hours.

The busiest railway station in the world is Clapham Junction. During the morning rush hour, 180 trains clatter through this station in south London.

HOUR 1

The latest printing presses are as tall as a house and can roll out 8.6 million pages in one hour. That is enough to make 90,000 newspapers.

HOUR 1

HOUR 1

A queen termite is the only member of a colony that lays eggs. She produces 1,250 eggs every hour.

QUESTION 1

How long did it take to cook the world's biggest omelette?

A: 6 HOURS
B: 23 HOURS
C: 2.6 HOURS

QUESTION 2

How long does it take to turn round a supertanker?

A: 1 HOUR
B: 14 HOURS
C: 3.5 HOURS

QUESTION 3

How long can a sperm whale stay underwater?

A: 4 HOURS
B: 13 HOURS
C: 1.5 HOURS

QUIZ

24

QUESTION 4

How much poo does the average person produce per hour?

A: 2KG   B: 360G   C: 18G

TRUE OR FALSE

Page 71: True
Page 79: False – It takes most radioactive waste 100,000 years to become safe.
Page 85: True
Page 93: False – Early TVs were bad for your eyes but modern ones are harmless.

QUESTION 5

How many hours did the longest tornado last for?

A: 20 HOURS
B: 3.5 HOURS
C: 9 HOURS

QUESTION 6

What is the world record time for climbing Mount Everest?

A: 2 HOURS, 40 MINUTES
B: 22.5 HOURS
C: 8 HOURS, 10 MINUTES

QUESTION 7

How many tomatoes are thrown during the one-hour Tomatina?

A: 150,000
B: 23
C: 2 MILLION

Answers 1: A: 6 hours, 2: A: 1 hour 3: C: 1.5 hours, 4: C: 18g, 5: B: 3.5 hours, 6: C: 8 hours, 10 minutes, 7: A: 150,000

Guy Laliberté, the Canadian billionaire who founded the famous Cirque du Soleil, paid £26 million for 11 days on the International Space Station. That's the most expensive holiday ever at £2.3 million per day.

DAYS **11**

 DAYS **3**

In 2011 the world's biggest meatball was cooked in Columbus, Ohio, USA, to celebrate the city's Italian Festival. It weighed as much as six men and took three days to cook!

Every 30 days, the people of the United States buy four billion bottles of water. If those bottles were laid end to end, they would go around the globe 16 times.

 DAYS **30**

New Zealanders are the biggest ice cream eaters on the planet. Every seven days the average Kiwi slurps ten scoops of ice cream.

7 DAYS

LICK 365

Modern military submarines can extract oxygen straight from seawater. It is a secret how long these boats can stay submerged, but most remain underwater for up to 90 days before coming to the surface for more supplies.

DAY 90

Radio

7 DAYS

The song 'You've Lost That Loving Feeling' by the Righteous Brothers was released in 1964 and has been played on the radio an average of 3,000 times every seven days since. That makes it the world's most played song.

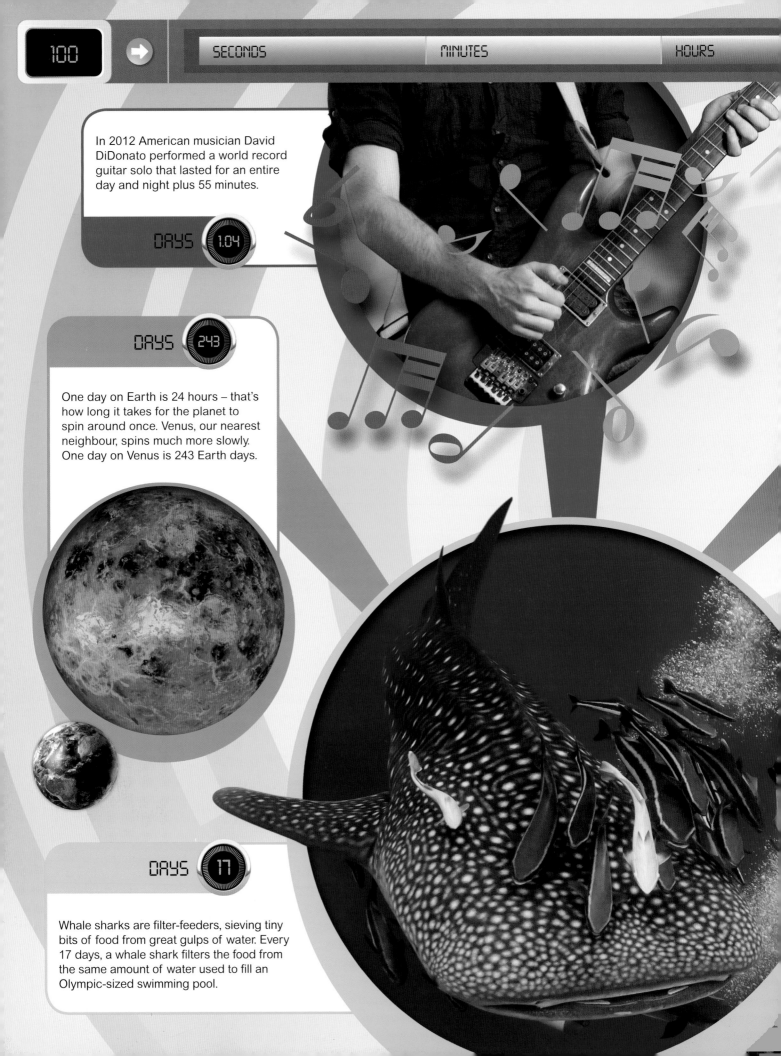

In 2012 American musician David DiDonato performed a world record guitar solo that lasted for an entire day and night plus 55 minutes.

DAYS   1.04

DAYS   243

One day on Earth is 24 hours – that's how long it takes for the planet to spin around once. Venus, our nearest neighbour, spins much more slowly. One day on Venus is 243 Earth days.

DAYS   17

Whale sharks are filter-feeders, sieving tiny bits of food from great gulps of water. Every 17 days, a whale shark filters the food from the same amount of water used to fill an Olympic-sized swimming pool.

159 DAYS

The 1984 World Chess Championship final lasted 159 days, making it the longest in history. Russians Anatoly Karpov and Gary Kasparov battled through 48 games in a row, and it ended in a draw!

In 2003 American illusionist David Blaine sat in a see-through box suspended above a London riverside park for 44 days without eating a single thing. He lost 24.5kg – about a quarter of his bodyweight.

DAYS 44

GULP!

365

1 DAY

The Three Gorges Dam in China is the world's largest power station. It has 32 electricity generators, which produce 540 gigawatts of power every day. However, that is still less than two per cent of all the power used in China.

The largest geothermal power station in the world is at Hellisheiði in Iceland. It uses the heat from volcanoes to produce electricity, and every day it provides 80 per cent of Iceland's homes with hot water.

DAY 1

POWER UP!

All of us need a power supply, to charge our phones, light our homes and cook our food. But how long does it take to produce and use?

 **1 DAY**

Shams 1 in Abu Dhabi is the largest solar power plant in the world. In one day it produces the same amount of energy as 15,000 car engines using the Sun – and it does it without producing any pollution.

True or false

A petrol-powered car can drive for about one day before it needs to refuel. An electric car can run for 16 days before it needs to be recharged.

(Answer on page 128)

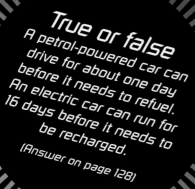

1 DAY

A modern fridge uses ten million joules of energy per day. Amazingly that is about the same as the energy in a healthy diet (2,400 calories a day).

1 DAY

The Druzhba pipeline, the world's longest, runs for 4,000km from Almetyevsk, Russia, to Schewdt, Germany. Every day, 1.4 million barrels of oil pump along it. That is the same volume that comes out of the River Thames in England every hour.

1 DAY

China has the most wind turbines of any country. The turbines can produce 6,500 trillion joules of energy in a day – enough to power a city 3.6 times the size of Shanghai.

The top layer of your skin is made of dead cells, which naturally fall off, especially during washing. It takes 28 days for the whole surface of your skin to drop off and be replaced with a fresh layer.

28 DAYS

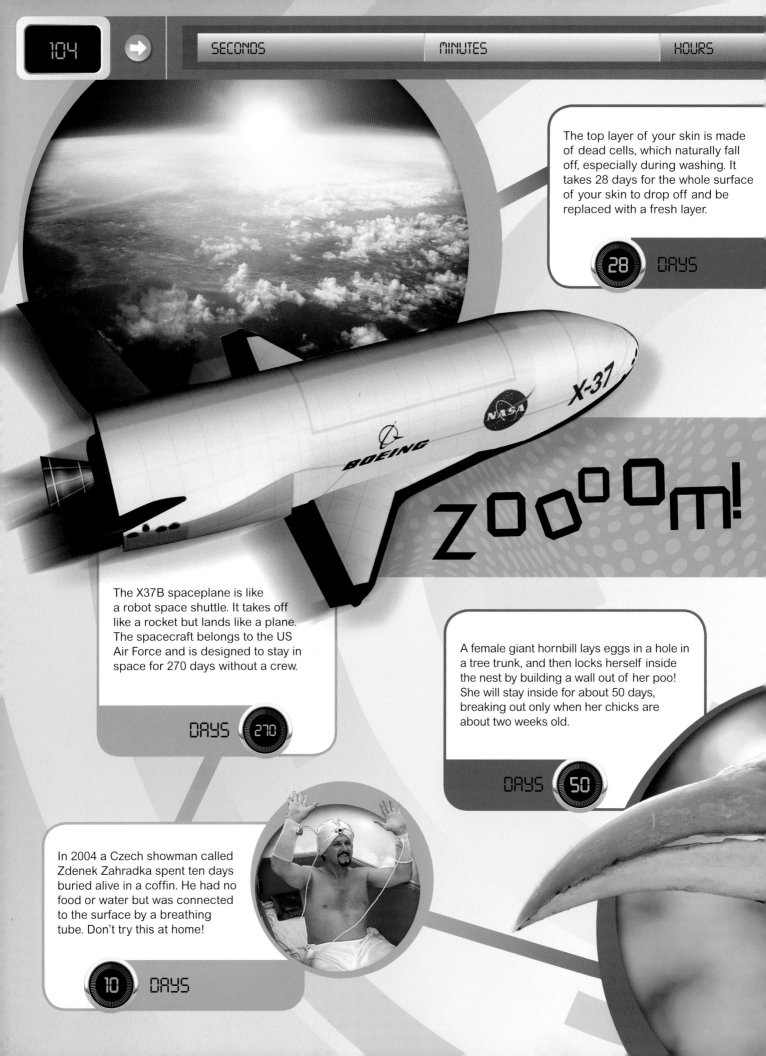

ZOOOOOM!

The X37B spaceplane is like a robot space shuttle. It takes off like a rocket but lands like a plane. The spacecraft belongs to the US Air Force and is designed to stay in space for 270 days without a crew.

DAYS 270

A female giant hornbill lays eggs in a hole in a tree trunk, and then locks herself inside the nest by building a wall out of her poo! She will stay inside for about 50 days, breaking out only when her chicks are about two weeks old.

DAYS 50

In 2004 a Czech showman called Zdenek Zahradka spent ten days buried alive in a coffin. He had no food or water but was connected to the surface by a breathing tube. Don't try this at home!

10 DAYS

Immense clouds of gas and dust out in space slowly collapse in on themselves until the squeezed middle ignites into a new star. Astronomers have calculated that about 275 million new suns are born somewhere in the Universe every day.

DAY 1

DAY 1

The biggest swing in temperature ever recorded in one day was at Loma, Montana, USA, on 15 January 1972. The low point was a frosty –47°C but this rose to 9°C later that day, a rise of 56 degrees.

DAY 1

Every day, 1.2 million cute little puppies are born around the world. That adds up to more than 400 million a year. The United States is the country with the most pet dogs – there are more than 75 million living there.

Turkish people are the biggest bread eaters in the world. The average Turk eats 1kg of bread every two days. That's more than half a loaf a day!

DAYS 2

Alpine marmots are the sleepiest mammals of all. In cold places they can hibernate in cosy burrows for 180 days a year.

DAYS 180

The average person yawns 15 times day. Nobody knows why we yawn – but it makes you feel sleepy just thinking about it.

DAY 1

DANCE!

365

 152 DAYS

The music video for 'Gangnam Style', the hit song by K-pop star Psy, was the first clip to clock up one billion views on YouTube. It took just 152 days, averaging around seven million views a day.

 1 DAY

The Tokyo subway is the world's busiest. Every day 6.3 million people take a ride beneath Japan's capital. Attendants squeeze people into the crowded carriages.

In 1929 the airship Graf Zeppelin flew around the world in 22 days (a record at the time). It took off from New Jersey, USA, on 7 August and visited Germany, Japan and Los Angeles before returning to the start on 29 August.

DAYS **22**

DAY **1**

The people of the world use just over 4.5 trillion cubic metres of water every year. That is an average of 1.75 cubic metres a day per person, enough to fill eight bathtubs.

WATER, WATER

Water is almost everywhere – including inside our bodies (we are two-thirds water). How much water is used on Earth every day? Dive in to see!

1 DAY

It takes 3.5 litres of water to produce one hamburger. Americans are the world-record burger eaters. They get through 36 million a day – and that requires 133 million litres, or 42 Olympic-sized pools, of water.

Cherrapunji in northern India is the rainiest place on Earth – more than 12m of rain fall every year. If you collected the rain that falls during 30 days (one month), it would be enough to fill four and a half buckets to the brim.

DAYS **30**

1 DAY

The tides roll in and out twice every day. The biggest tides in the world are at the Bay of Fundy in eastern Canada, where high tide is 17m higher than the low water mark. That's the height of three giraffes.

DAY **1**

Every day, 37 billion litres of water plunge over the Inga Falls. This waterfall on Africa's River Congo has the biggest volume of water. All that water would be enough to fill 7,490 supertankers.

DAY **1**

The Amazon is the world's longest and largest river. It runs right across South America and carries a fifth of all Earth's river water. Every day it releases 1.8 trillion litres into the Atlantic Ocean.

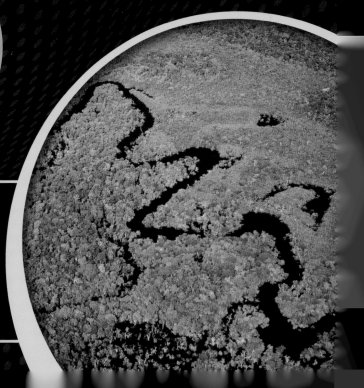

DAYS 31

The longest lasting hurricane was Typhoon John in 1994. The superstorm lasted 31 days and travelled 13,800km from its starting point off the west coast of Mexico to the Aleutian Islands in the North Pacific.

1 DAY

Every day of the year, 93,000 passenger jets are cleared for take off with a total of 7.5 million passengers on board. Over a year that adds up to a third of everyone on Earth taking a trip by plane.

365

FLY!

DAYS 5

The Golden Temple in Amritsar, India, is the most visited building in the world. Every five days, around 100,000 people go into this magnificent Sikh shrine, which is more than India's most famous monument, the Taj Mahal.

On 14 August 2010, the traffic on China's Highway 110 from Beijing to Mongolia ground to a halt. The hold-up lasted until August 23 – ten days later. Most drivers spent at least five days stuck in the queues.

10 DAYS

A standard pencil is 19cm long. Every six days enough pencils are made to join end-to-end all the way around the Earth.

6 DAYS

It takes an African elephant five days to eat one tonne of food. That is the same as 2,000 boxes of cereal.

5 DAYS

DAYS 25

The average person's hair grows 1cm every 25 days. That is the length of a thumbnail.

In 2008 New Zealander Mike Heard broke a world record by making 103 bungee jumps off Auckland Harbour Bridge in just one day. In total he fell more than 4km.

DAY 1

If you buy a ticket from Moscow, Russia, to Pyongyang, North Korea, you had better take a book to read on the way. At 10,214km, this is the longest rail journey in the world, and it takes 189 hours or 7.9 days – with just three stops in between.

DAYS 7.9

The Kumbh Mela is a Hindu religious festival, where believers bathe in a sacred river in Allahabad, India. In the 2013 event, 40 million people went to take a dip over 55 days.

DAYS 55

An ant is one tough bug. In one day, it can walk 1,090m. Considering the ant is only 0.5cm long, that is the equivalent of a man walking 381km in the same amount of time. (The average human can manage less than a tenth of that: 32km per day.)

DAY 1

SPLISH SPLASH!

365

10 DAYS

In the very hottest desert conditions camels can go for ten days without a drink, and a lot longer when the weather is cooler. Camels survive thanks to their humps, which are filled with oily fats.

Before the invention of four-wheel drives the quickest way to cross the Sahara Desert was by camel. It takes 52 days to ride a camel from Timbuktu, Mali, south of the desert to Marrakesh, Morocco, in the north.

DAYS 52

DAYS 57.5

In January 2008 Francis Joyon arrived in the port of Brest, France, in his trimaran IDEC 2. He had just spent the last 57.5 days sailing around the world all by himself – setting a new world record.

TIME TO TRAVEL
Super fast or super slow – there are loads of ways to move around the globe.

40.7 DAYS

In 2012 Briton Penny Palfrey swam 112km between Grand Cayman and Little Cayman in the Caribbean in one day, 16 hours and 41 minutes – the longest solo ocean swim ever.

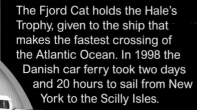

The Fjord Cat holds the Hale's Trophy, given to the ship that makes the fastest crossing of the Atlantic Ocean. In 1998 the Danish car ferry took two days and 20 hours to sail from New York to the Scilly Isles.

DAYS 2.8

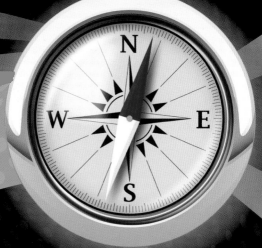

In 1911 Norwegian Roald Amundsen became the first person to reach the South Pole. His team then walked, sledded and skied back to base, covering the round trip of 3,440km from the coast to the frozen Pole and back in just 99 days.

DAYS 99

9 DAYS

In December 1986 Dick Rutan and Jeana Yeager took off from California and landed there again nine days later – after flying around the world! Their aircraft, the Rutan Voyager, is the only aircraft to have flown all the way around the world on one tank of fuel.

True or false

In 2013 the flight time from the Russian space centre to the International Space Station was reduced from two days to just six hours. That is quicker than flying from London to New York.

(Answer on page 128)

365

VOILA!

36 DAYS

The Swiss are the world's biggest chocolate eaters. They eat 1kg of it (or about 17 snack bars) every 36 days.

1 DAY

Paris is visited by more tourists than any other city on Earth. Every day 74,000 people look at the city's charming sights – and nearly all of them go to the Eiffel Tower.

1 DAY

In April 1921 Silver Lake, Colorado, USA, became a real winter wonderland. A total of 192cm (or two-thirds of the way up a basketball hoop) of snow fell in just one day.

DAYS 90

Babies spend 280 days growing inside their mothers. Many of their body features take only a few weeks to develop. For example, after 90 days, the tiny human already has a unique set of fingerprints.

DAY 1

The average dairy cow produces 24 litres of milk every day – enough for 192 bowls of cereal.

DAYS 5

It takes five days to assemble an iPad – and 325 people to carry out each step in the process.

DAY 1

The west coast of North America is fringed with a giant kelp forest. These huge seaweeds are the fastest-growing plants on Earth. They grow 60cm in one day. That is 240 times faster than grass.

The Yukon 800 is the longest speedboat race in the world, and runs for two days straight. The course is 1,285km along the Yukon River in Alaska, USA, which is like travelling from Rome to Paris.

DAYS 2

365 Brrrrr!

 7 DAYS

Every year, the average worker spends a total of seven days just travelling to work and coming home again.

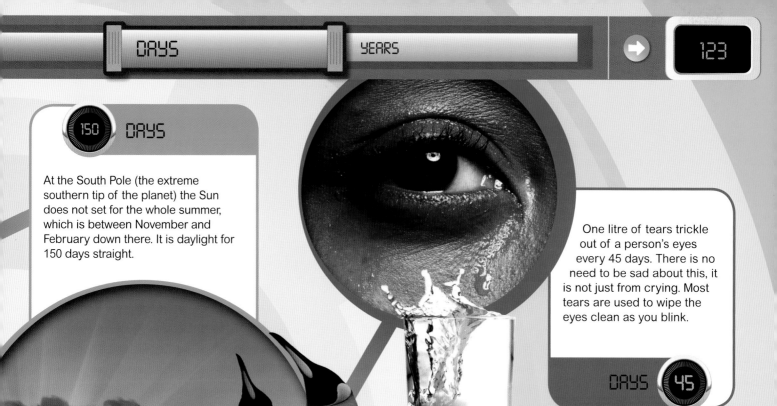

150 DAYS

At the South Pole (the extreme southern tip of the planet) the Sun does not set for the whole summer, which is between November and February down there. It is daylight for 150 days straight.

One litre of tears trickle out of a person's eyes every 45 days. There is no need to be sad about this, it is not just from crying. Most tears are used to wipe the eyes clean as you blink.

DAYS 45

DAYS 101

In 1947 six Norwegian adventurers led by Thor Heyerdahl set sail from the west coast of Peru in South America on a wooden raft. It took 101 days for the flimsy craft to cross the Pacific Ocean – the distance from Anchorage, Alaska, to Washington, DC, in the USA.

Greeks eat 2.5kg of cheese every 30 days – more than any other country. That is the weight of a pack of printer paper every month!

DAYS 30

Thirty-three miners were trapped when a mine in Chile collapsed in 2011. Rescuers took 69 days to rescue them, and all 33 hold the record for surviving the longest mining accident.

DAYS 69

DAYS 6

Every year the world's toughest runners take part in the *Marathon des Sables* (Marathon of the Sands) in the rocky desert of Morocco. Competitors run 251km – the distance of six marathons – in six days.

MIND AND BODY

Time to get tough! For some of these amazing people, survival and endurance is all in a day's work. But a strong mind and body is required for all.

3.2 DAYS

Arulanantham Suresh Joachim from Sri Lanka holds the record for standing on one foot. In 1997 his second foot did not touch the ground for three days and four hours.

14.5 DAYS

In 1977 Maureen Weston of England stayed awake for a record-breaking 14.5 days. She achieved this feat while taking part in a rocking chair marathon. Maureen just kept rocking day after day, night after night without a wink of sleep. She must have slept well afterwards!

True or false
The longest drum solo lasted for 19 days. So many people complained about the noise that police in Lisburn, Northern Ireland, eventually made the drummer stop.

(Answer on page 128)

DAYS 286

In 2005 three shark fishermen ran out of fuel off the west coast of Mexico. They floated for 286 days – the longest time adrift in a boat – until they were rescued near the Marshall Islands on the other side of the Pacific.

In 1992 Australian hiker James Scott became lost in the mountains of Nepal. He survived for a record-breaking 42 days without food before being rescued.

42 DAYS

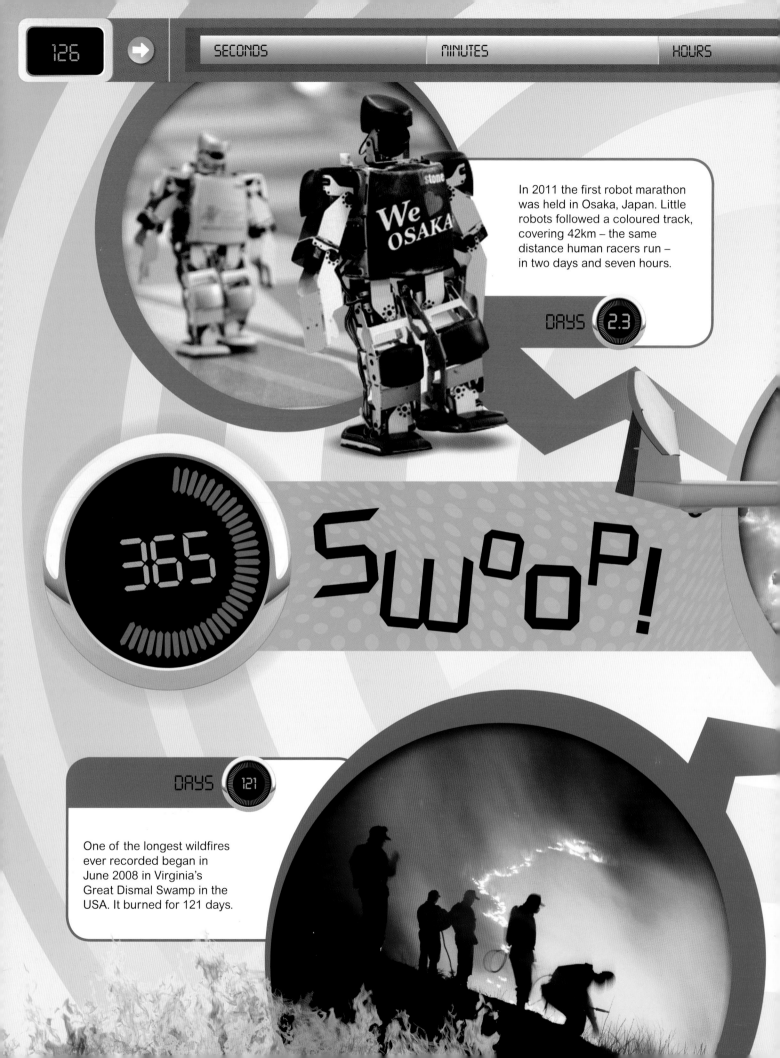

In 2011 the first robot marathon was held in Osaka, Japan. Little robots followed a coloured track, covering 42km – the same distance human racers run – in two days and seven hours.

DAYS 2.3

365

SWOOP!

DAYS 121

One of the longest wildfires ever recorded began in June 2008 in Virginia's Great Dismal Swamp in the USA. It burned for 121 days.

2.3 DAYS

French pilot Charles Atger holds the record for the longest glider flight. In 1952 he stayed in the air without the aid of an engine for 2.3 days.

Eyelashes protect the eyes, keeping bugs and grit out. They fall out as new ones grow. You get a completely new set of eyelashes every 150 days.

DAYS 150

The wood frog lives in the far north of Canada, where the winters are very cold. When the frogs hibernate their bodies freeze solid for at least 28 days – probably more. This is the only frog that can survive being frozen.

DAYS 28

'Candle in the Wind', a charity song by Elton John in honour of Diana, Princess of Wales, is the fastest selling single in history. In just seven days, four million copies were bought.

DAYS 7

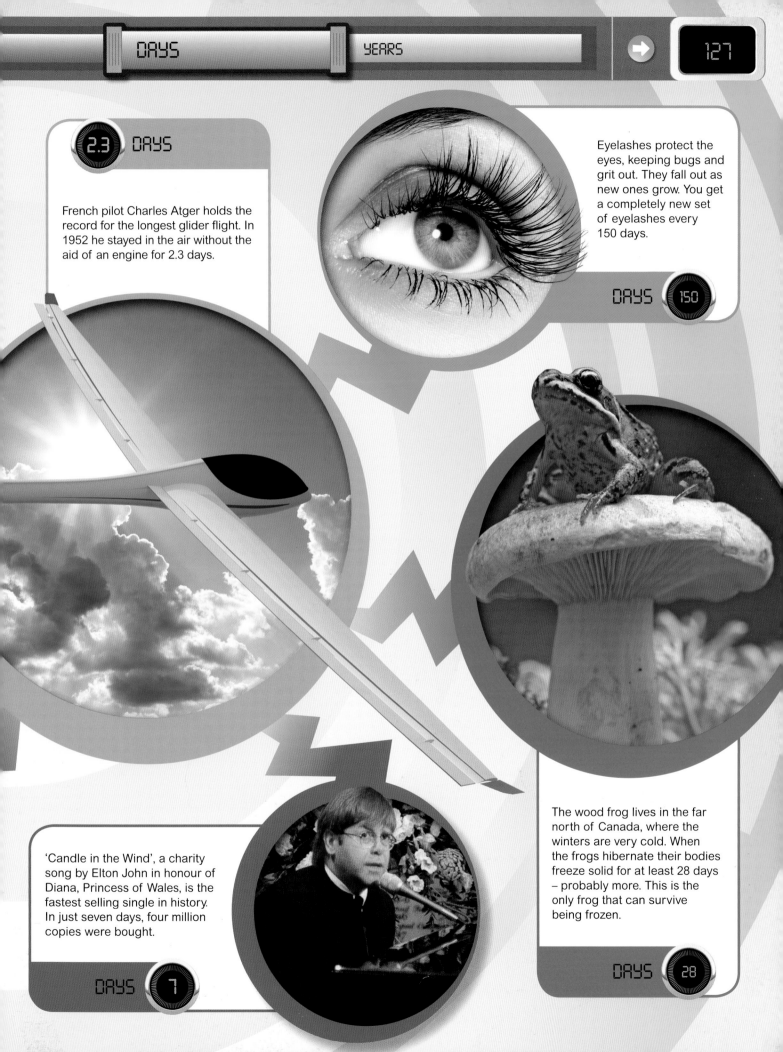

QUESTION 1

How much did Guy Laliberté's 11-day holiday in space cost?

A: £25.50
B: £72 BILLION
C: £26 MILLION

QUESTION 2

About how long does it take for the average Swiss person to eat 1kg of chocolate?

A: THEY NEVER EAT IT
B: 36 DAYS
C: 20 MINUTES

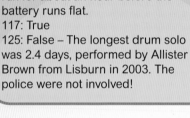

QUESTION 3

How long did it take for one billion people to watch the 'Gangnam Style' YouTube video?

A: 6 MINUTES
B: 2 DAYS
C: 152 DAYS

QUESTION 4

How long did it take Dick Rutan and Jeana Yeager to fly around the world?

A: 4 HOURS
B: 9 DAYS
C: 2 WEEKS

TRUE OR FALSE

103: False – Most electric cars can run for about an hour before the battery runs flat.
117: True
125: False – The longest drum solo was 2.4 days, performed by Allister Brown from Lisburn in 2003. The police were not involved!

365 QUIZ

QUESTION 5

How long does the sun stay in the sky during summer at the South Pole?

A: 150 DAYS
B: ALL THE TIME
C: IT NEVER RISES

QUESTION 6

How many dogs live in the United States?

A: 75 MILLION
B: 453,000
C: 2 BILLION

QUESTION 7

How many new stars form every day?

A: 275 MILLION
B: 8 MILLION
C: 4

Answers 1: C £26 million, 2: B 36 days, 3: C 152 days, 4: B 9 days, 5: A 150 days, 6: A 75 million, 7: A 275 million

26 YEARS

Australian Graham Barker has the largest collection of navel fluff in the world. He's been collecting it for 26 years and it weighs 22.1g – the weight of a mouse.

10 YEARS

The deepest hole ever dug went 12.2km into the ground. That is 3.5km deeper than Mount Everest is tall. It took ten years to drill it in western Russia. The rocks at the bottom of the hole were as hot as an oven.

Navel Fluff 1984 - 1993

Navel Fluff 1994 - 2000

Navel Fluff 2001 -

YEARS 1.2

Russian cosmonaut Valeri Polyakov holds the record for staying in space. In the mid-1990s he spent 437 days (1.2 years) as a crew member of the Mir space station.

The longest time a human body has stayed alive is 122.4 years. The body belonged to Frenchwoman Jeanne Louise Calment who was born in 1875 and died in 1997.

YEARS 122.4

GrOss!

100

Ngwenyama Sobhuza II became Paramount Chief of Swaziland at the age of just four months in December 1899. He remained on the throne until August 1982, a total of 82.7 years. That is the longest reign in history.

82.7 YEARS

Golden Jubilee of KING SOBHUZA II

SWAZILAND

 3.5 YEARS

In 1963 an underwater volcano erupted off the coast of Iceland. Over the next 3.5 years, an island of lava grew out of the boiling sea, forming a new island named Surtsey. In that time it grew to almost half the size of Manhattan.

Niger has the highest birth rate of any country. Every year 80,000 new citizens are born – that's one baby for every 21 Nigeriens.

1 YEAR

1.25 YEARS

In 2011 Paul Archer, Leigh Purnell and Johno Ellison took the most expensive cab ride in history – driving around the world in a London taxi. The meter clocked up an £80,000 cab fare during the journey, which lasted one and a quarter years and visited 50 countries.

100

TAXI!

Hic!

Hic!

Hic!

Hic!

American Charles Osborne had the longest attack of hiccups on record. He hiccupped for 68 years from 1922 until 1990.

YEARS 68

In 1704 Scottish sailor Alexander Selkirk was marooned on an island off the coast of Chile for 4.3 years. His story inspired the book *Robinson Crusoe*, and now the Chilean island is named after him.

4.3 YEARS

198 YEARS

Pluto's summer lasts for 50 years, when it is near enough to be warmed by the Sun. For the next 198 years, Pluto plunges into winter, which is so cold that even its atmosphere freezes!

Lake Vostok

4km of ice

Lake Vostok is covered by 4km of ice in Antarctica. Experts think that the lake, which is around the size of Lake Ontario, has been isolated from the rest of the world for 15 million years.

15 MILLION YEARS

The average person in Japan lives to be more than 83 years old, the highest age of any country.

YEARS 83

1 YEAR

In 2011 gutsy Dutch runner Stefaan Engels ran 365 marathons – or one marathon every day for a year. That's a total jog of 15,3400km or more than a third of the way around the globe.

In the 2001 Major League season, Barry Bonds of the San Francisco Giants hit 73 home runs, a record that has not been beaten since.

YEAR 1

YEAR 1

French rally driver Sébastien Loeb was hard to beat in 2008. He won 11 of the 15 races that year – a record-breaking feat.

WINNING TIMES
Top sports stars are in it to win. And some are triumphant time after time. Take a look at some of the biggest winners around.

Helen Wills, an American tennis player, had a six-year winning streak, the longest ever. Between 1927 and 1933, Wills did not lose a single match, not even a single set!

 6 YEARS

Mancil Davis, a professional golfer from Texas holds the record for holes-in-one in pro tournaments. In a 15-year career between 1974 and 2007, Mancil scored a total of 51 aces.

YEARS 15

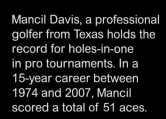

21 YEARS

The Brazilian football legend Pelé scored the most goals of any player. In 21 years and 1,363 professional matches, he scored 1,280 goals – a record-breaking average of 0.94 goals per game.

True or false
South African chess players Reinhart Straszacker and Hendrickvan Huyssteen played chess by post from 1946 to 1999. They played 112 games in that time – the match ended in a draw: 56 games all.

(Answer on page 156)

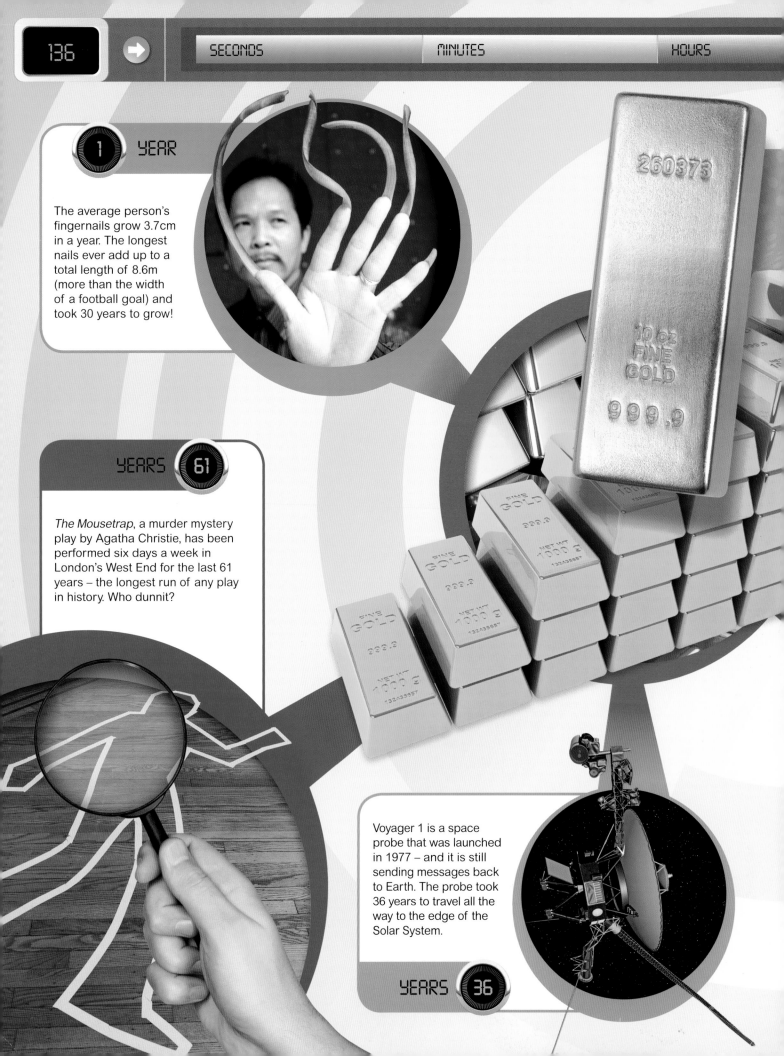

1 YEAR

The average person's fingernails grow 3.7cm in a year. The longest nails ever add up to a total length of 8.6m (more than the width of a football goal) and took 30 years to grow!

YEARS 61

The Mousetrap, a murder mystery play by Agatha Christie, has been performed six days a week in London's West End for the last 61 years – the longest run of any play in history. Who dunnit?

Voyager 1 is a space probe that was launched in 1977 – and it is still sending messages back to Earth. The probe took 36 years to travel all the way to the edge of the Solar System.

YEARS 36

BLING!

100

YEAR 1

Every year 2,500 tonnes of gold is dug out of mines. That's about the same weight as over 600 full-grown hippos!

25 YEARS

Marco Polo is famous for travelling from Venice, Italy, to China, where he lived with the emperor Kubla Khan. He was away on his epic journey for 25 years.

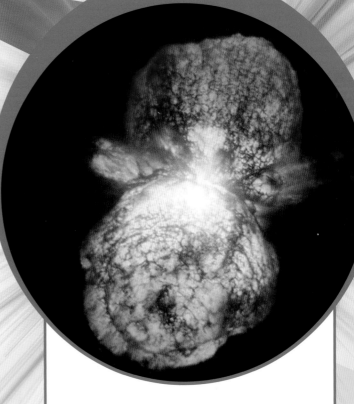

When giant stars die they go out with a very big bang. The explosion is called a supernova, and they are quite rare. Astronomers have calculated that there is a supernova every 50 years in our galaxy. The last one was in 1985.

YEARS 50

2600 YEARS

The Stromboli volcano forms a small island off the coast of Sicily. People have been recording its activity for centuries, and Stromboli has been erupting more or less constantly for the last 2,600 years – longer than any other volcano. Most of the time it belches out ash and smoke, but lava also pumps out every now and then.

YEAR 1

Every year, 24 million hectares of wheat are grown in the United States. That is enough to cover the whole of the United Kingdom.

FLAP

100

YEARS 40

Puya raimondii, a plant that lives in the Andes Mountains in South America, blooms only every 40 years. However, its flower is an amazing 10m high when it does!

1 YEAR

In 2012 around 60 million new cars were made. It is predicted that there will be two billion cars on the world's roads by 2030.

In 1804 Meriwether Lewis and William Clark led an expedition to explore the west of the United States. The explorers set off from St Louis, Missouri, and they arrived on the West Coast 1.5 years later.

YEARS **1.5**

1 YEAR

The Arctic tern has the longest migration of any animal. Every year it flies a total distance of 70,000km on a round trip from the Arctic to the Antarctic and back again.

LEWIS AND CLARK TRAIL

Every year, the people of Brunei eat 245kg (or about 1,189 cupfuls) of rice each – three times as much as the world average. That is the same weight as 1,255 sandwiches!

1 YEAR

WE WILL BUILD IT

They're tall, huge and impressive. The world's most amazing buildings took some time to construct. But just how long?

14 YEARS

The most famous building in Australia is the Sydney Opera House. The curved concrete roof is supposed to look like sails and took 14 years to build. The opera house was opened in 1973.

The world's tallest building is Burj Khalifa in Dubai. It is 829.8m high, which is taller than the Empire State Building, Chrysler Building and Statue of Liberty stacked on top of each other. It took six years to erect.

YEARS 6

19 YEARS

In 1993 Pudong was a swamp across the river from Shanghai, China. In 19 years it was turned into a modern high-rise city, home to more than five million people – and more buildings are planned.

140 YEARS

The Basilica di Santa Maria del Fiore, the magnificent cathedral in Florence, Italy, is better known simply as the Duomo. It took 140 years to build and the last bit to be added was the huge dome, which is made from bricks and held together with huge iron chains.

2 YEARS

The Millennium Dome was built to celebrate the year 2000. It took two years to put up and was built with time in mind. The dome is 365m wide, one metre for every day of the year. There are also 12 pillars for each month.

No one knows how the Great Pyramid of Egypt was built, but the best guess is that it took 40,000 workers 20 years to put its 2.3 million stone blocks together in 2540BCE.

YEARS 20

True or false
The Sagrada Família in Barcelona, Spain, took just one year to build, the fastest time a cathedral has been completed.

(Answer on page 156)

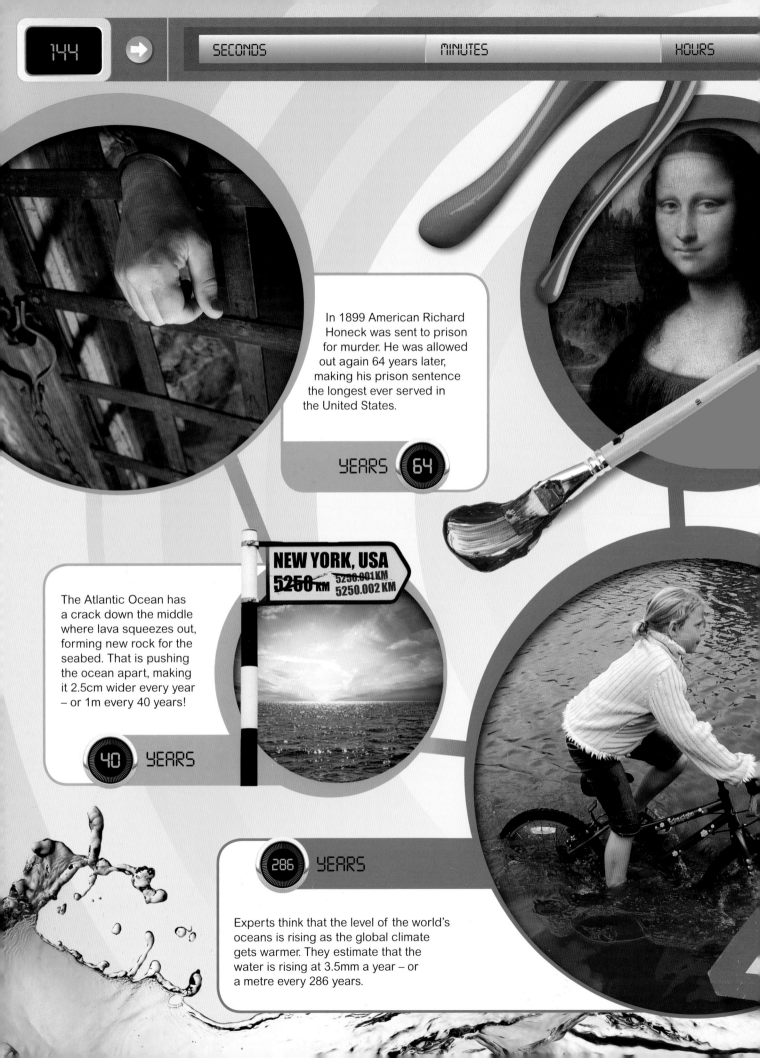

In 1899 American Richard Honeck was sent to prison for murder. He was allowed out again 64 years later, making his prison sentence the longest ever served in the United States.

YEARS 64

NEW YORK, USA
5250 KM 5250.001 KM
         5250.002 KM

The Atlantic Ocean has a crack down the middle where lava squeezes out, forming new rock for the seabed. That is pushing the ocean apart, making it 2.5cm wider every year – or 1m every 40 years!

40 YEARS

286 YEARS

Experts think that the level of the world's oceans is rising as the global climate gets warmer. They estimate that the water is rising at 3.5mm a year – or a metre every 286 years.

YEARS **4**

The *Mona Lisa* is one of the most famous paintings in the world. It took Italian artist Leonardo da Vinci four years to finish it in 1507.

American Dave Kunst was the first person to walk all the way around the world (apart from ocean crossings). It took him four years in the 1970s, walking 23,255 km or 20 million paces.

4 YEARS

In winter, the Arctic Ocean freezes into 15 million sq km of ice – twice the area of Australia. In spring it starts to melt and shrinks to a piece of ice with an area of 3.5 million sq km – about the size of India.

YEAR **1**

Flood Zone

FLOOD!

100

2.5 MILLION YEARS

The Andromeda Galaxy is our near neighbour in space. It it a bit bigger than our galaxy, the Milky Way, with around a trillion stars. The light from these stars takes 2.5 million years to reach Earth. The light used to make this photograph left the galaxy when our early ancestors were just learning how to make stone tools.

The Panama Canal cuts through a narrow strip of Central America to connect the Atlantic with the Pacific. It took 11 years to dig the 77km waterway, which divides North America from South America.

YEARS **11**

100

MUMMY!

11 YEARS

The Sun can get spots (dark areas on the surface formed by the star's magnetic field). The number of spots follow a regular cycle lasting 11 years, where sunspots first grow in number and then disappear again.

30 YEARS

No one knows her name, but the wife of Russian Feodor Vassilyev had the most children ever. Over 30 years in the mid-1700s she had 69 children, including 16 pairs of twins, seven sets of triplets and four sets of quadruplets.

The Centennial Light is a light bulb at the fire department in Livermore, California, USA. It has been on more or less constantly for the last 110 years, making it the longest-lasting light bulb in the world.

YEARS 110

10 YEARS

India is moving north, crunching against the rest of Asia – and that is what is pushing up the Himalayas (Earth's biggest mountains). Mount Everest and other mighty peaks rise another 5cm every ten years.

Halley's comet is one of the brightest comets to fly past Earth. It comes by every 76 years on its way around the Sun. It is due back in 2061.

YEARS 76

Lonesome George was the last Pinta giant tortoise, a species from the Galápagos Islands. He lived for more than 100 years before dying in 2012. For at least 41 of those years he was the rarest animal on Earth.

YEARS **41**

17 YEARS

Periodic cicadas live underground, sucking sap from roots for 17 years. Only then do they all climb up to the surface, grow wings and find a mate. It is harder for predators to time an attack on all those bugs at one time.

GROWING UP

Girls stop growing around the age of 15, while boys keep going for another four years or so. How long does it take for other animals to grow up?

25 YEARS

Quahog clams live in cold seas and grow very slowly. Most reach a full size of 9cm after 25 years, but they never stop growing – some quahogs are thought to be more than 475 years old!

True or false

After two years lemming fur gets very long and itchy. The rodents search for water to soothe their itch and are so desperate they will leap from cliffs to reach the sea.

(Answer on page 156)

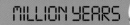

MILLION YEARS 0.7

The Great Barrier Reef runs for 2,500km along the coast of Australia. It took 700,000 years to grow, built up from layer after layer of the shells left by billions of tiny coral polyps.

1 YEAR

Rabbits can have babies at the age of three months. That means a rabbit can become a great-grandparent before its first birthday!

African elephants are the biggest land animals on Earth. They are 50 times bigger than a human but they reach adult size in just 15 years.

15 YEARS

100

STRETCH!

3500 YEARS

In 1519 Portuguese explorer Ferdinand Magellan set off to sail around the world but he was killed in the Philippines. His second-in-command, Juan Sebastián Elcano, completed the first circumnavigation of the globe in just under three years.

The world's biggest trees are the giant sequoias of western North America. The oldest ones are 3,500 years old and have been growing since Tutankhamun was pharaoh of Egypt!

YEARS 3

3 YEARS

A rhino's horn never stops growing throughout its life. If the horn is cut off it will grow back again to full size (about 1m long) in around three years.

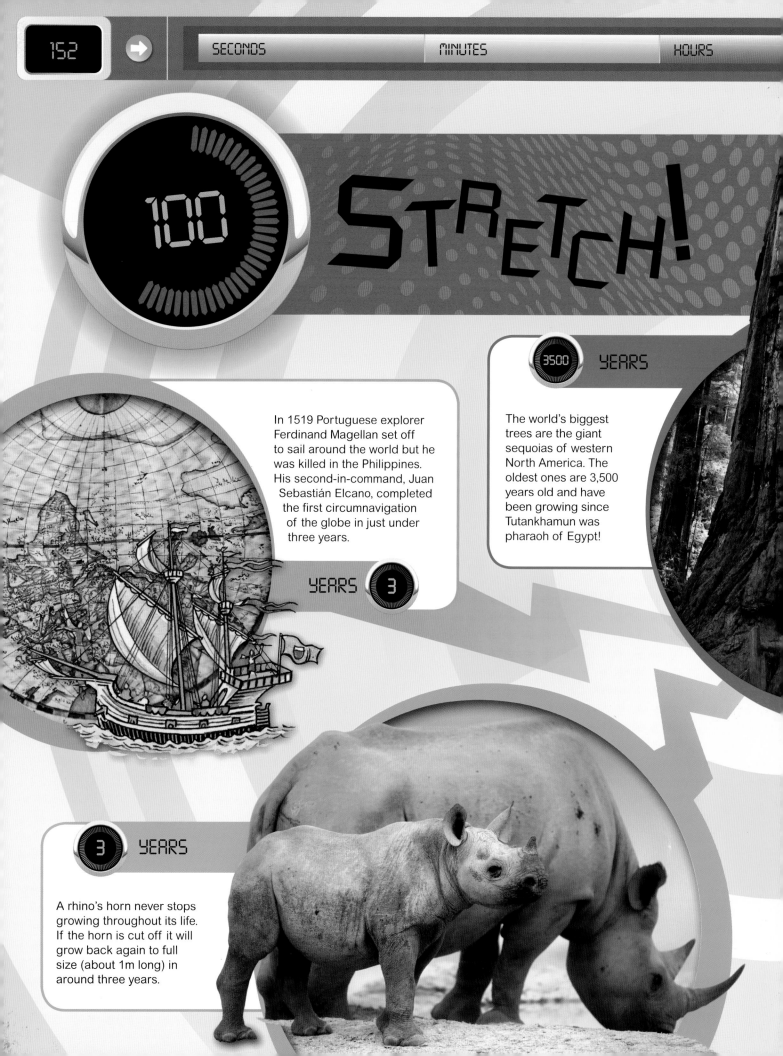

YEARS **7**

The Black Death arrived in the Crimea, on the eastern corner of Europe, in 1346. Seven years later it had spread across the continent as far as Norway and Ireland and killed half of everyone in Europe – about 100 million people.

YEARS **5**

The Three Gorges Dam in China blocks the Yangtze River, forming a 600km-long lake. It took five years for the lake to fill up to its full depth of 175m, and it covered the homes of 1.4 million people who moved out to make way for it.

The Opportunity robot has been rolling around Mars for more than nine years, helping NASA to study the red planet. That makes it the longest serving rover ever. It does get the winter off though – the Martian sunlight is too weak to charge its batteries.

YEARS **9**

Bill and Laurel Cooper from Britain decided to sail around the world in 1976 – and they just kept going for 36 years, going round the world four times. This is the record for the longest time living on a boat.

YEARS 36

YEAR 1

On average six people are killed by sharks every year. Unfortunately 100 million sharks are killed by humans in a year – mostly for their fins.

In 1964 Canadian animator Richard Williams started work on a film called the *Thief and the Cobbler*. It took him 29 years to finish. It was finally released in 1993, making it the longest production time of any film.

YEARS 29

British author Barbara Cartland holds the record for writing the most novels in one year. In 1983 she wrote 23 books – almost one every two weeks. In total Barbara wrote 723 books and sold a billion copies.

YEAR 1

The human population is growing fast! In just 47 years the number of people on Earth has doubled to today's figure of more than seven billion.

47 YEARS

EXTINCT

1 YEAR

Biologists have recorded more than one million species but estimate that there are about 40 million in total. Every year 40,000 species become extinct – mostly before anyone has recorded them.

SNACK TIME!

100

QUESTION 1

How long did it take to drill the world's deepest hole?

A: 230 YEARS
B: 10 YEARS
C: 40 DAYS

QUESTION 2

How far does an Arctic tern fly every year?

A: IT CAN'T FLY
B: 3 MILLION KM
C: 70,000 KM

QUESTION 3

How long has the Stromboli volcano been erupting?

A: 95 YEARS
B: 2,600 YEARS
C: 456 YEARS

QUIZ

QUESTION 4

How many home runs did Barry Bonds hit in the 2001 baseball season?

A: 145 B: 0 C: 73

TRUE OR FALSE

Page 135: True
Page 143: False – The church was started in 1882 and it will not be completed until at least 2026!
Page 151: False – Lemmings jumping off a cliff is a myth, based on a nature documentary from 1958 where lemmings were filmed being thrown off a cliff!

QUESTION 5

How long did it take Leonardo da Vinci to complete the *Mona Lisa*?

A: 27 YEARS
B: 4 YEARS
C: 20 MINUTES

QUESTION 6

How many blocks are there in the Great Pyramid?

A: 2.3 MILLION
B: 22 MILLION
C: 66,000

QUESTION 7

The longest attack of hiccups lasted for...

A: 68 YEARS
B: 3 DAYS
C: 14 YEARS

Answers 1: B 10 years, 2: C 70,000km, 3: B 2,600 years, 4: C73, 5: B 4 years, 6: A 2.3 million, 7: A 68 years

INDEX

PICTURE CREDITS

Interior: All images Dreamstime, istockphoto, Shutterstock and Thinkstock, except:
10c, Mike Kemp/Rubberball/Getty Images; 10br, Jane Sweeney/ JAI/Corbis; 10–11, Visuals Unlimited/Corbis; 11tr, Pictorial Press Limited/Alamy; 11bl, Reuters/Corbis; 11br, Gotoenter at en. wikipedia; 13cl, NASA; Jon W. McDonough/Sports Illustrated/ Getty Images; 15cr, Photo Huanqiu.com; 15br, Courtesy Barbie. com; 19tr, David White/Alamy; 19bl, Ardo/Public Domain; 19br, Johan Bueno/EricBarone/Tu Diversion; 22tl, Jason Richards/ Public Domain; 27tr, Medio Tuerto/Getty Images; 27b, US Army; 34tl, CBW/Alamy; 36tl, Public Domain; 39bl, M. & C. Gilfedder/ Vireo; 40l, Kay Nietfeld/EPA; 41b, Jebulon/Public Domain; 42–43, Corbis; 45br, Ferrari World Abu Dhabi; 48tr, NASA; 48b, NASA; 50tl, NASA; 51cr, Robert Hunt Library; 53bl, David Taylor/Getty Images; 53tr, NASA; 54l, Martin Oeser/AFP/Getty Images; 54t, Courtesy Serginho Laus; 54b, Fabrice Coffrini/AFP/Getty Images; 56–57, Waltraud Grubitzsch/DPA/Corbis; 60br, Robert Hunt Library; 61c, Victor Boyko/Getty Images; 61t, Stephen Vaughan/ Paramount Pictures/Kobal Collection; 62b, Courtesy David Mullins; 63b, Tasos Katapodis/Stringer/Getty Images; 63r, Jeff Rotman/Alamy; 67bc, Paul Souders/Corbis; 72tl, Splash News/ Corbis; 72bl, Miguel Salmeron/Getty Images; 74–75, Reinhard Dirscherl/Getty Images; 76tr, ESA; 80, NASA; 81b, Harald Sund/ Getty Images; 82l, SSPL/Getty Images; 83b, Philip Dalton/Nature Picture Library; 86l, RIA Novosti/Topfoto; 86b, Kevin Foy/Alamy; 86–87t, Zuma Press/Alamy; 87tr, Emmanuel Aguirre/Getty Images; 90tr, The Print Collector/Alamy; 93bl, Sipa Press/Rex Features; 93tr, Everett Collection/Rex Features; 93b, Xavier Arnau/Getty Images; 94b, Boston Dynamics; 95tr, Dan Kitwood/ Getty Images; 95br, Chuck Mason/Alamy; 98c, John Wellings/ Alamy; 98t, Alexander Nemenov/AFP/Getty Images; 99br, Michael Ochs Archives/Getty Images; 101tr, Ian Patrick/Alamy; 102t, Xiao Yijiu/Xinhua Press/Corbis; 104t, NASA; 104bl, mydailynews.com; 105tr, NASA; 108r, Jeff Dravitz/Film Magic/Getty Images; 109bl, The Print Collector/Alamy; 109br, Horizons WWP/Alamy; 110tl, Ross Woodhall/Getty Images; 111t, AFP/Getty Images; 111br, Will & Deni McIntyre/Getty Images; 116tr, Courtesy Penny Palfrey; 117t, The Print Collector/Alamy; 117r, Universal Images Group/ Getty Images; 117bl, NASA; 122tl, Zuma Press/Alamy; 123bl, Courtesy Kon-Tiki Museum; 124tl, Christophe Dupont Elise/Icon SMI/Corbis; 124t, Gobierno de Chile/Public Domain; 125tl, Stephen Chiang/Getty Images; 125c, Mike Parry/Minden Pictures/FLPA; 125br, Jimmy Chin/Aurora Photos/Corbis; 126tl, AFP/Getty Images; 127b, AlamyCelebrity/Alamy; 130cl, NASA; 130c, AlamyCelebrity/Alamy; 130br, George Gobet/AFP/Getty Images; 131b, FLPA/Alamy; 134tl, Kevin Rushforth/Public Domain; 135tl, Art Rickerby/Time Life Pictures/Getty Images; 136tl, Chen Kang/Image China/Corbis; 136br, NASA; 140tl, Andrew Sacks/Getty Images; 144–145b, Daniel Berehulak/Getty Images; 146–147, NASA; 148tl, Library of Congress; 149br, NASA; 150t, Mark Putney/Public Domain; 152–153, Radius Images/Alamy; 153t, Public Domain; 153r, NASA, 153b, Stringer Shanghai/Reuters/Corbis; 154–155t, Poras Chaudhary/Getty Images; 155b, David Gleetham/Visuals Unlimited/Corbis.

Every effort has been made to acknowledge the source and copyright holder of each picture. The publishers apologise for any unintentional errors or omissions.